MANUFACTURED HOMES

MANUFACTURED HOMES

Making Sense
of a Housing Opportunity

THOMAS E. NUTT-POWELL
MIT-Harvard Joint Center for Urban Studies

 Auburn House Publishing Company
Boston, Massachusetts

Library of Congress Cataloging in Publication Data

Nutt-Powell, Thomas E., 1944–
  Manufactured homes.

  Bibliography: p.
  Includes index.
  1. Prefabricated houses. 2. Prefabricated houses—
United States. I. Title.
HD7287.5.N87   338.4′769397   81–14846
ISBN 0–86569–086–3   AACR2

The First One, to Bonnie

FOREWORD

Manufactured housing has often been touted as a wave of the future, only to remain stuck with its past—a sales system and legal status descended from the auto and trailer business, and a stubbornly unattractive reputation with many households.

Today, however, manufactured housing is receiving renewed attention, and proponents now include a substantial proportion of federal, state, and local housing professionals. Observers recall that pre-cut homes were once negatively compared to site-built dwellings, but this early distinction has now all but disappeared. By the same token, there are predictions that the distinctions between manufactured housing and "stick-built" homes will also disappear, particularly as design and siting improvements render them increasingly similar.

Tom Nutt-Powell gives a clear and detailed picture of an industry and a concept in transition. He documents the emergence of a truly nationwide housing industry and, as evidence, cites research by the U.S. Department of Housing and Urban Development on durability problems of manufactured homes (which he calls MHs, a useful contraction that also accommodates the former term "mobile home"). The author notes that HUD's specific conclusions and recommendations on avoiding damage due to transportation and set-up are exceedingly important, because they could be required by HUD in the design of every new MH in the nation.

The MH industry's support for the enactment of national standards, incidentally, is an example of a consistent, long-held, and farsighted policy. California's 1957 statewide mobile home construction standards, the first in the nation, were instigated and supported by industry. Here, at least, is one example of regulation that has benefitted virtually everybody concerned.

The author has collected some of the best recent research on the

vii

question of MH quality, and the results are encouraging. Fire safety has improved dramatically under the national standards, and for recently built units is now equal to or better than for conventional dwellings. Wind damage can be largely avoided with proper underpinnings and tiedowns (a conclusion we, in California, have also reached with respect to earthquake damage).

Previous national publications on MHs by authors outside the industry have tended to treat them as an interesting, but exotic and possibly dangerous, new development. Nutt-Powell concludes, with evidence, that MHs are in practical terms "as good as" any other form of housing. This is in itself a major step forward.

Where do we go from here? The book's agenda is sound: Work on the image, on financing, on better tax and titling systems, and on eliminating discriminatory land use restrictions. California has taken several steps recently to implement this kind of agenda, and to bring MHs into a "head-to-head" competitive stance with site-built homes. These include state laws to:

- Tax all new MHs as real property instead of as vehicles;
- Prohibit discrimination against MHs on residentially-zoned land (while allowing some local control over placement and appearance);
- Allow the removal and recycling of MH wheels, hubs, axles, and tow bars;
- Exempt MHs from most sales tax;
- Expand allowable MH height and width limits for highway travel;
- Transfer all MH administrative matters from the Department of Motor Vehicles to the Department of Housing and Community Development; and
- Include MHs as eligible under California's numerous housing grant and loan programs.

However, much more work needs to be done on MH multistory and townhome configurations, particularly in California, as increasing land costs dictate higher densities and more intensive use of precious residential sites.

The question remains, however: How will homebuyers react as MHs gradually approach equality with conventional housing in access to land and financing? The author predicts that in the near term, although MHs may claim practical equivalence, they will remain "rarely the first choice of housing consumers." However, with continued improvements, this may change over the long term.

The dark side in California of the advance of MHs into a new niche in the market is the doubtful future of mobile home parks. Too many parks originally built on fringe land are now prime sites for more intensive forms of development, and today's fringe land is often protected for agricultural purposes. An intensifying shortage of park spaces has led to more frequent allegations of rent gouging; to the sad spectacle of elderly tenants with old mobile homes, virtually unplaceable in other parks, being evicted due to park conversions; to several local park rent control ordinances (which may dampen developer perceptions of the return on investment for new parks); and to the Mobilehome Residency Law being the fastest-growing subspecies of landlord-tenant law in California statutes.

It all adds up to accelerated evolution under pressure. The future will be better for it, but not without loss and unexpected side effects. In manufactured housing, as in so many other fields, the 80's will be a pivotal time. This book provides an illuminating status report.

I. DONALD TERNER
Director, Department of Housing
and Community Development
State of California

PREFACE

It was late 1964. I was about to complete my undergraduate degree at Penn State, and had accepted a job at a state hospital near Altoona. At that time Altoona was still suffering from the ravages of being almost entirely dependent on the Pennsylvania Railroad. The economy was far from vibrant, the housing stock severely deteriorated. The apartments I looked at in my price range (and, as desperation set in, even above it) were old, badly maintained, and unappealing; the neighborhoods by and large matched the qualities of the housing. I bemoaned this plight to a soon-to-be colleague, who suggested contacting a departing staff member about renting her "trailer" in a park about a half mile from the hospital. Taking a "why not!" attitude, I looked, and liked what I saw.

The compact unit (about 420 square feet) included a living/dining room, kitchen, bath with shower/tub, and bedroom. Though it was a Central Pennsylvania winter day, the house was warm and, with its wood paneling, cozy. The $40/month rent made it most attractive to my starting budget, even with heat and utilities added on. I moved in, and found that living there was just fine. Indeed, when the first staff member took a position at a California hospital, I "moved up" by buying his "mobile home." It was bigger, about 576 square feet, with an eat-in kitchen, a large living room, a paneled study, a much larger bathroom, and a large bedroom with sliding-door closets. My monthly housing costs about doubled, but I was "building equity" and had a much more comfortable home.

I left Altoona for a job at the Baltimore Urban Renewal and Housing Agency and the next step in my personal housing career. Since leaving Altoona I have lived in a basement apartment, a garden apartment (with private balcony!), a manse in Maryland horse country, a Baltimore row house, triple-deckers in both Cambridge and Boston, a semi-detached "worker" house in one of Sam Bass Warner's "street car suburbs," a house with a porch and fireplace of Roxbury puddingstone, a large apartment in a 1920s apartment building, and now, a big old Victorian perched on the side of Corey Hill in Brookline, just up from Boston's famous trolley line.

Until about four years ago I hadn't given much thought to those first two homes in Altoona. They had been pleasant to live in. They had been much better than anything else available, even at twice the price. In short, they had met my needs.

But then, in 1977, I got a request from the Massachusetts Department of Community Affairs. Could a student team do a study of the role of mobile homes in meeting Massachusetts' housing needs? I said yes, as it seemed a good chance to provide my planning students the opportunity to do a complete housing policy analysis, covering market demand and need, design and construction, costs, legal issues, and the general question of public acceptance of housing policy recommendations. Since my experience with this housing form had been positive and, from my perspective, rather ordinary, I naively assumed that this sort of study could proceed essentially like any other housing study. I was wrong. Instead, the students kept returning with complaints of data inadequacies and an absence of information on how other states and localities dealt with this king of housing. They also reported being met with awkward silences, if not overt snickering, as a response to inquiries about what they were working on.

I did some looking myself and found, like the students, essentially nothing (except, of course, a modest kind of derision.)

Since this was after the imposition of the HUD Code which, I supposed, did what other housing codes do—establish a uniform (and acceptable) level of construction quality—this void seemed unnecessary. I posed this problem to Arthur Solomon, then Director of the Joint Center for Urban Studies of MIT and Harvard University, who had just finished a stint on HUD's Low-Cost Housing Task Force. He also felt that the general lack of knowledge about this kind of housing in the shelter industry meant many missed opportunities. We resolved to correct this situation, and put together a formal research effort.

What you are about to read is a product of that effort. Its roots are in my interest in having good information for policy and program formulation in the shelter industry. Since the public and private sector components of that industry are mutually dependent, I have attempted to make this book useful to both audiences. Those without much prior knowledge about MHs—how they are built, their quality, who builds and finances them, and who lives in them—will find Chapters 2–4 especially helpful. Those who do not know much about public sector treatment of MHs (whether at local, state, and/or federal levels) will find useful information in Chapters 5 and 6. Anyone with some interest in making use of this housing opportunity will find that Chapter 7 identifies some of the current dilemmas, as well as proposes some approaches to sorting them out.

The current and future housing needs of this country are not to be laughed at, not with the high cost of money added to the high cost of building. Manufactured homes present a real opportunity to meet many of those housing needs. It is my hope that this book helps make sense of that opportunity.

T.E.N.-P.
November 1981
Boston

ACKNOWLEDGMENTS

This book was made possible by the assistance of literally hundreds of individuals. I am very grateful to each of them for their willingness to spend time, on numerous occasions, in response to my questions.

I would especially like to acknowledge the support of Arthur Solomon, former Director of the Joint Center, who was enthusiastic in his support of my proposals for research in this area; Bill Weide, a member of the Joint Center's Policy Advisory Board, who facilitated the initial grant to get the research started; and my colleagues and friends, Michael Furlong and John Zeisel, who, by sharing with me their thoughts on housing in general and manufactured homes in particular, have made mine better.

CONTENTS

LIST OF TABLES

LIST OF FIGURES

MANUFACTURED HOMES

Chapter 1

INTRODUCTION

The crux of the U.S. housing crisis is cost—the housing that people want costs more than they can afford. As costs of housing continue to mount, the median price of a new single-family site-built house exceeds the buying power of an ever-larger segment of our population. Attempts to provide solutions have met with limited success, whether based on supply-side theories (for example, public housing or mortgage subsidies) or demand-side policies (housing allowances or tax deductions and credits).

Manufactured homes, because of their apparently lower costs, would seem to hold some hope for meeting the housing needs of at least a portion of our society. Because these homes are built to a single national construction and safety code administered by the Department of Housing and Urban Development (HUD), they are, in the housing policy litany, "decent, safe, and sanitary."

Yet this form of housing, though providing no fewer than 200,000 units annually for the past decade, does not appear to be attracting the expanding consumer reception one might expect, given cost differentials from other types of housing. To what can we attribute this relatively limited use of manufactured homes? Are there ways for the public and/or private sector to prompt expanded use of manufactured homes, and good reasons for doing so? This book responds to these questions.

Overview

This book is divided into three sections. The first section, comprising Chapters 2 through 4, examines the construction, marketing, and buyers of manufactured homes. Chapter 2 considers the

1

production of these homes and presents current assessments of their quality. The process by which manufactured homes reach their markets is reviewed in Chapter 3, as well as descriptions of the traditional and changing roles of manufacturers, dealers, transporters, financers, and trade organizations. Chapter 4 discusses housing market issues pertinent to manufactured homes, including characteristics of residents of these homes, determinations of cost and value, trends in market activity, and notable consumer concerns.

The second section of the book (Chapters 5 and 6) reviews attitudes and actions of the public sector toward manufactured homes. Chapter 5 looks specifically at state and local issues, including housing policies and programs, legal and tax status, ownership recording practices, and the nature and changing applications of development controls. Chapter 6 presents a similar review at the federal level, considering the activities of agencies directly involved in housing provisions such as HUD and the VA, agencies with indirect involvement such as FNMA and FHLBB, and agencies with a consumer protection interest, such as the FTC.

The third section and final chapter of the book assesses the role of manufactured homes in the current housing crisis. It sets forth the issues requiring attention if sensible use is to be made of this housing opportunity.

The remainder of Chapter 1 defines the terms used to provide a basis for understanding contemporary manufactured homes in relation to other housing forms.

Definition of Manufactured Housing

Manufactured housing is a generic term describing housing produced in a factory rather than at the actual site. The distinction between manufactured and site-built housing is not rigid, however. Manufactured housing requires varying amounts of site work, while certain parts of site-built housing (roof trusses or pre-assembled/prehung windows and doors, for example) may be manufactured.

There are two types of manufactured housing. The first type is built to state-adopted building codes that, in turn, are based on national or regional model codes, such as the Uniform Building Code (UBC). Included in this first type are precut or shell homes, components, panelized homes, modular or sectional homes, and so on, for which the degree of product completion in the factory (as opposed to completion at the site) varies greatly. For manufactured housing built to state codes, the National Association of Home Manufacturers has nine product classifications based on the differences in the extent of completion at the factory, on construction style, and on use of the manufactured structure.[1]

The second type of manufactured housing is built to a single national standard embodied in the federal Manufactured Home Construction and Safety Standards, which are administered by the U.S. Department of Housing and Urban Development (HUD). This single, preemptive national standard is known as the HUD Code.

Manufactured housing built to the HUD Code is often referred to as a "mobile home"—a name resulting from its evolution from the travel trailers of the '30s and '40s. This terminology, however, is inaccurate. A more structurally precise designation is "mobile-component housing," a term highlighting the structural distinctiveness of this form of manufactured housing—namely, three-dimensional components that are intrinsically mobile. An integral structural element of each component of a house built to the HUD Code is a wheeled chassis. Although the axle, wheels, and connecting "tongue" can be removed, the two I-beams of the chassis remain a basic structural element.

Most mobile-component houses are structurally complete on leaving the factory, with all four walls, floor, and roof completely joined. However, about one third of recently produced mobile-component houses consist of two or more "mobile-components," each comprising three walls, roof, and floor. The two or more components are then joined at the site. All mobile-component houses require connection to appropriate services and facilities at the site, and many have structural additions such as porches and garages made on site. Though it is technically feasible to move a mobile-component house (assuming retention of wheels, axle, and tongue for each component), the contemporary reality is that there is only one move, from the factory to the site.[2]

Mobile-components are built to widths that conform to maximum permissible highway loads. Since most states permit loads up to 14 feet wide on their highways, this is the most frequent component width. Hence width control led to the industry terms *single-wides*—referring to a structurally complete, single-compo-

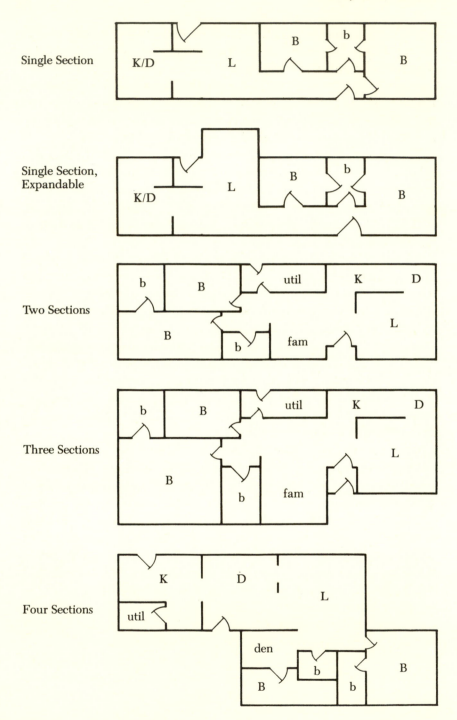

Figure 1-1 Typical MH Floor Plans.

Figure 1–2 Contemporary Multisection Manufactured Home. *(Photo courtesy of the Immobile Home Co.)*

nent, mobile-component house—and *double-* (or *multi-*) *wides*—referring to mobile-component houses of two or more components. This width-based terminology is being replaced by the designations *single-section* and *multisection*. Figure 1–1 shows various combinations of components, including a two-component, mobile-component house in which the second component is a small expansion of the living room.[3] Figures 1–2, 1–3 and 1–4 illustrate the interiors and exteriors of contemporary mobile-component houses.

Figure 1–3 Contemporary Single-Section Manufactured Home. *(Photo courtesy of Fleetwood Enterprises.)*

Figure 1–4   Interior of a Contemporary Manufactured Home. *(Photo courtesy of the Immobile Home Co.)*

Although the designation *mobile-component housing* is structurally accurate, it is awkward for common usage. And, though the mobile-component house is but one of many possible forms of single-family detached dwellings, its structural heritage does necessitate a distinction in policy and program analysis. For purposes of this book, therefore, the current congressional designation *manufactured home*, or *MH*, will be used.

Notes

1. NAHM (1980, pp. 66–67) defines the nine classifications in the following way: (1) precut and/or shell homes; (2) components; (3) panelized homes; (4) mechanical or utility cores; (5) modular or sectional homes; (6) log homes; (7) geodesic dome homes; (8) multifamily homes; and (9) commercial structures.
2. Mobility has dramatically decreased in the recent past due to the increased number of multisection MHs and the increased size of single-section MHs. Recent data suggest that only 1 to 3 percent of MHs are moved other than from factory to site.
3. A slight exception to the basic definition, this second component is not itself mobile, but is carried within the first. Such a two-section MH is referred to as an "expandable."

Chapter 2

MH: THE HOUSING UNIT

In this chapter the actual manufacturing process for MHs is described and the unique attributes of constructing housing in this manner are discussed. The regulation of MH construction by the HUD Code, as well as a summary of HUD's five-year research program on MHs, including results pertinent to the quality of MHs, is presented. Finally, the HUD Code is compared with codes for other single-family dwellings.

MH Construction: Unique Attributes

The factory construction of MHs to the HUD Code yields three unique characteristics of MH production: worker skill requirements, the timing of production, and economies of scale.

Worker Skill Requirements

The construction of MH and site-built housing involves many similar building processes. However, the regularity with which any given process occurs in the construction of an MH permits the training of crews to repeat only certain tasks, and to repeat them under factory-supervised conditions. This task simplification means that any given worker need not be skilled in a trade, per se. Rather, the worker need only acquire skills necessary for the assigned task. When changes in unit design require a new set of tasks, workers are trained for the new tasks; no necessary, *a priori* generic and transferable skills are presumed. The factory location, assembly-line construction approach and task-specific skill requirement are reflected in the *industrial* unionization of employees in the MH industry. By comparison, those working in site-built housing construction tend to have a trade union affiliation.

Construction Timing

Because MH construction occurs indoors, it can proceed independent of weather conditions at a regular and predictable production rate. Thus management control is further simplified, and labor incentives can be keyed to demonstrable task-linked productivity. Nonseasonal production also means that the wage structure need not account for extended periods of unemployment due to inclement weather.

Economies of Scale

The National Association of Home Builders estimated that in 1980 there were 127,000 builders, with 40 percent of them building ten or fewer units per year. By comparison, in 1980 about 180 firms were building MHs at approximately 420 factory sites (MHI, 1981a). The average number of MH units produced per plant in 1980 was 651. Thus, even for firms with but a single plant, considerable economies of scale are realized in materials purchase alone, and economies are even greater for firms with many plants. Design and construction to a single national code minimizes the administrative time spent in obtaining regulatory approvals from multiple jurisdictions (state and local). Volume production allows for task specialization at the management as well as the construction level. Furthermore, large firms develop financial sophistication and can obtain more favorable treatment from lenders for both short-term cash and long-term capital formation needs.

MH Construction Process

The contemporary MH construction plant tends to be a single-story, slab foundation, "manufactured" metal building. The assembly line is straight, U-, or L-shaped, with storage and sub-assembly areas alongside. MH sections move along the assembly line either end-to-end or side-by-side. Figure 2–1 presents a typ-

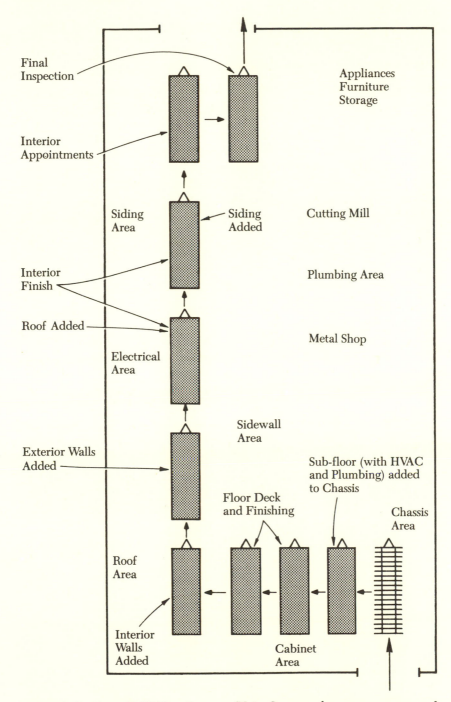

Figure 2–1 Typical MH Plant Layout. (Note: Some work areas are on a second level.)

Table 2–1   Labor Consumption by Component for a Typical 980 sf Single-Section MH

Component	Person-Hours	Item
Chassis/wheels	8.20	Chassis, wheel/axle assembly (excluded: heating, plumbing, electrical)
Floor	10.20	Framing members, subfloor, underflooring insulation, vapor barrier (excluded: floor finish, heating, plumbing, electrical)
Exterior wall	12.30	Framing members, exterior siding, interior paneling, insulation, vapor barrier (excluded: wall finish, heating, plumbing, electrical)
Roof	13.60	Framing members, trusses, exterior roof and subroof, ceiling insulation and vapor barrier (excluded: ceiling finish, ventilation fans, electrical)
Interior partitions	5.40	Framing members, paneling (excluded: wall finish, heating, plumbing, electrical)
Doors and windows	3.40	Fixed and operable window units, exterior and interior door units
Exterior finish	.40	Exterior painting, shutters, gutters and downspouts, other exterior trim and ornamentation
Interior wall finish	6.10	Interior painting, wallpaper, vinyl wall covering, baseboard, other wall trim
Floor finish	2.30	Linoleum and vinyl flooring, carpeting and pad
Ceiling finish	.90	Ceiling tile, planks, panels, plaster or painted ceiling
Heating and ventilating	3.80	Furnace, exhaust fans, heating ducts, grilles and registers (excluded: air conditioner)
Plumbing	7.90	Hot water heater, water supply system, drainage/vent system, bath and kitchen fixtures, gas system
Electrical	10.10	Distribution panel, circuit breaker, wiring, switches and outlets

Table 2–1 (cont.)

Component	Person-Hours	Item
Kitchen equipment	24.80	Range, range hood, refrigerator, kitchen sink, cabinets, other storage, counter tops (excluded: disposal, dishwasher)
Bathroom equipment	1.10	Bathtub and shower, watercloset, lavatory, medicine cabinet, lavinette
Furnishings	11.90	Furniture, beds, lamps, drapes
Delivery	6.00	Assume 100 miles delivery distance
Total	128.40	

SOURCE: Bernhardt, Arthur D., with the assistance of Susan A. Comando and Herbert B. Zien. 1980. *Building Tomorrow: The Mobile/Manufactured Housing Industry.* Cambridge, Mass.: MIT Press, p. 125.

ical plant layout, with the MH units moving end-to-end on an L-shaped assembly line.

MHs are constructed from the bottom up and the inside out. The typical elapsed time from a chassis first entering the assembly line to the completion of an MH section is one to three working days, depending on plant activity and unit specifications. Table 2–1 presents person-hours spent on construction of the various structural elements for a typical 14 foot by 70 foot single-section manufactured home.[1] Various structural elements are constructed at subassembly stations, then added to the MH unit at the appropriate point on the assembly line. Figure 2–2, identifying the construction specifications, is an exploded drawing of a two-section MH.

The first step in the assembly process is to attach the chassis, complete with axles and wheels, to the subfloor frame. This frame, complete with utility lines, heat ducts, and insulation, is fastened to the chassis with lag bolts.[2] Figure 2–3 illustrates this step.

The next step is installation of floor plumbing and flooring. Carpeting and/or vinyl flooring are laid, with cutouts made for heating, plumbing, and mechanical equipment. (See Figure 2–4.)

The installation of various interior components is the next assembly step, at which are added interior walls, cabinets, appliances, plumbing fixtures, furnace, water heater, and special interior features such as wood-burning fireplaces. Interior wall

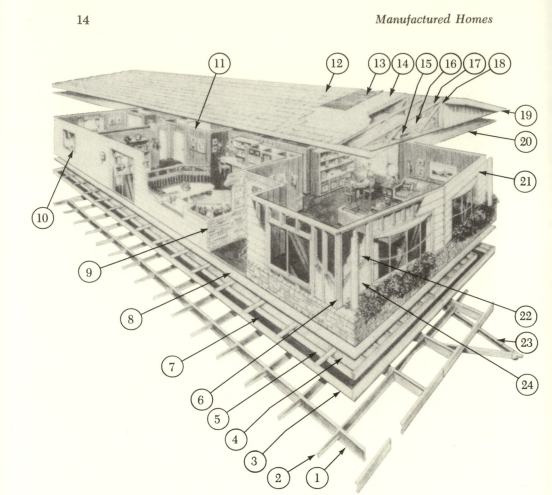

1. Heavy duty I-beam frames
2. Outriggers and cross members
3. Rodent-proof bottom board material
4. 3½" R-11 fiberglass insulation
5. 2 × 6 Floor joists
6. Studs spaced 16" on center on exterior walls
7. Perimeter air return system
8. 5/8" Sub-floor
9. Decorative brick or stone accent
10. House type sliding windows and removable screens
11. Studs spaced 16" on center in interior partitions
12. Fiberglass shingle roof
13. Two layers 15 lb. felt
14. 3/8" Plywood sub-roof
15. Overhead heating and cooling with 5/8" fiberglass ducts
16. 7" R-22 fiberglass insulation, ceiling
17. Truss-type roof rafters spaced 16" on center
18. Plywood ridge beam
19. Front overhang eave
20. ½" Tongue and grooved acoustical-type plank ceiling with ply veneer backing
21. House-type horizontal siding with 3/8" backing
22. Stress-rated plywood throughout
23. Detachable hitches
24. 3½" R-11 fiberglass insulation

Figure 2–2   Construction Specifications. (*Source: Silvercrest Industries.*)

Figure 2–3   Floor Frame on Chassis. *(Photo courtesy of William F. Allan.)*

Figure 2–4   Finish Flooring Installation. *(Photo courtesy of William F. Allan.)*

sections and cabinets are built at a subassembly location. Often, the walls are wired and finish paneling or gypsum wallboard are affixed prior to movement of the section to the assembly line. This stage is illustrated in Figure 2–5.

One or more exterior walls may be installed prior to completion of the interior. Similarly, exterior walls, often including both necessary wiring and insulation, are constructed at a subassembly

Figure 2–5 Interior Wall Installation. *(Photo courtesy of William F. Allan.)*

station. Fastener plates and metal straps are used to secure the joints where walls are attached to the floor frame, roof frame, or other wall frames. (See Figure 2–6.) High-compression nailing and stapling machines are used in this construction step. After all exterior walls are installed, the final interior work is completed: Overhead cabinets are installed; electrical work is finished, except for ceiling connections; and doors, molding, closet fixtures, and other finish items are completed.

The next stage of the assembly line is the installation of the ceiling/roof component, which is constructed at a subassembly station, often with wiring and insulation. It is then positioned on and attached to the exterior walls; wiring is completed, and, if necessary, insulation installed. A relatively recent design change to the traditional metal roof has been the use of pitched, compo-

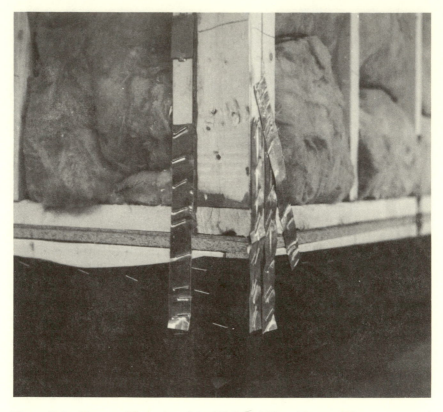

Figure 2-6   Fastener Plates Attaching Walls and Floor Frame. *(Photo courtesy of William F. Allan.)*

sition shingle roofs, on both single-section and multisection MHs. (See Figure 2-7.)

The use of a variety of siding materials—aluminum, steel, wood, and stucco—in various textures and colors has changed the external appearance of the contemporary MH. The installation of the siding, often over an exterior insulating sheathing, indicates the near completion of the MH unit. Figure 2-8 illustrates this step.

The next to last step on the assembly line is completion of both interior and exterior trim work and addition of various interior appointments. The unit then receives a complete inspection, including utilities, and necessary repairs and adjustments are made. The MH unit is then ready for shipment, the last in-plant construction step. (See Figure 2-9.)

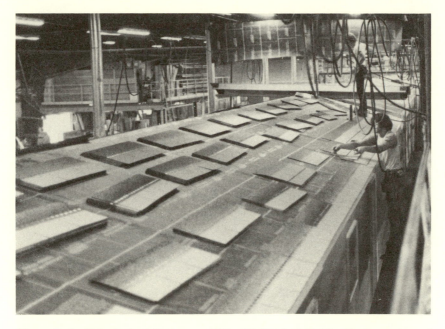

Figure 2-7 Shingle Installation on MH with Pitched Roof. *(Photo courtesy of William F. Allan.)*

Figure 2-8 Siding Installation. *(Photo courtesy of William F. Allan.)*

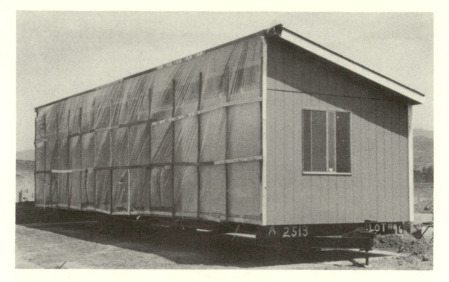

Figure 2–9   One Section of a Manufactured Home Prepared for Shipment. *(Photo courtesy of Fleetwood Enterprises.)*

MH Construction Regulation

In 1974 Congress approved legislation providing for a single, pre-emptive set of construction and safety standards for MHs. The U.S. Department of Housing and Urban Development (HUD) was given responsibility to establish and enforce these standards. To fulfill its responsibilities, HUD created an Office of Mobile (now Manufactured) Home Standards. Initially responsible to the Assistant Secretary for Housing Production and Mortgage Credit, the OMHS was transferred to the Assistant Secretary for Consumer Affairs and Regulatory Functions (later Neighborhoods, Voluntary Associations and Consumer Protection) in 1976. In 1981 responsibility for administration of the 1974 act was returned to HUD's Assistant Secretary for Housing.

The HUD Code became effective June 15, 1976.[3] The code, derived in large part from a set of voluntary industry standards adopted under ANSI procedures, covers the design and construction process. It also establishes certain requirements pertinent to provision of information to MH consumers and response to consumer complaints regarding construction defects.

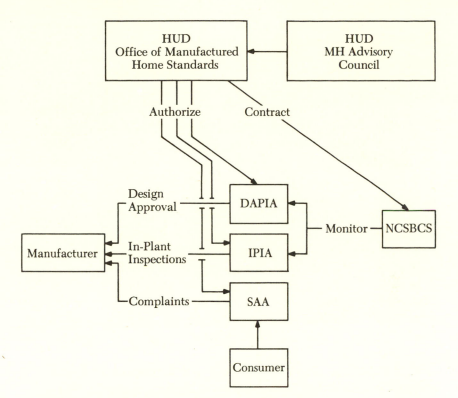

Figure 2–10 Administrative Structure of HUD's MH Construction and Safety Standards Program.

HUD administers its MH Construction and Safety Standards decentrally, as shown in Figure 2–10. Two types of agencies carry out primary inspections. First, a design approval primary inspection agency (DAPIA) reviews all manufacturer designs and specifications to assure conformance with the HUD Code; the DAPIA also reviews manufacturer quality control programs. Second, an in-plant primary inspection agency (IPIA) certifies that a manufacturer is capable of producing DAPIA-approved units in compliance with the HUD Code. The IPIA also inspects at least one part of each MH to determine if the unit is being constructed in conformance with the standards. The IPIA will issue the required HUD label only on a positive finding. DAPIAs are always private firms, although IPIAs may be either a private firm or a state agency. Both IPIAs and DAPIAs must be approved by HUD.

A state administrative agency (SAA) handles consumer complaints, makes enforcement-related determinations, conducts hearings, and may, on HUD's approval, serve as an exclusive IPIA for its state. SAA functions in states that have chosen not to participate in the HUD program are performed by HUD.

Under contract with HUD, the National Conference of States on Building Codes and Standards (NCSBCS) monitors the activities of IPIAs and DAPIAs. A per-unit fee collected by NCSBCS funds NCSBCS monitoring functions and certain SAA activities. In addition, manufacturers pay fees for DAPIA and IPIA services.

Finally, HUD has established a National MH Advisory Council to serve as a forum for discussion of MH construction and safety standards. Its 24 members provide equal representation for MH industry, consumer, and public sector interests.

During 1978 and 1979, SAAs received between two and four complaints for every 100 MH units produced each month, or between 500 and 800 complaints monthly (HUD, 1980, pp. IV–40, 41). HUD classified about one half of the complaints as "structurally" caused, primarily defective doors, floors, and windows (HUD, 1980, pp. IV–19, 20).

In addition to HUD's regulatory and consumer activities, the Federal Trade Commission has been active regarding MH sales and warranty service. In 1972 the FTC began an industrywide investigation of MH manufacturer warranty practices. Consequently, in December 1974, four manufacturers entered into consent orders in which they agreed to institute specific procedures to improve their warranty service. At the same time the FTC proposed a rule-making proceeding. A final report and proposed rule was issued in August 1980 (FTC, 1980). (The nature of the FTC's investigations and proposed regulations will be discussed at greater length in Chapter 6.) It is sufficient for present purposes to note that its activities, and especially the consent decrees (which involved three of the six largest MH producers), provided certain constraints on manufacturer activities, however indirect.

MH Quality: HUD Research

As part of its responsibilities to improve the safety and quality of MH construction, HUD has undertaken research on a variety of topics. The combination of the single national code and the large amount of research completed in a relatively·short period of time makes it possible to say much about the technical performance of this housing form. The following sections summarize HUD research conducted between 1975 and 1980 pertinent to MH quality, including durability, fire, wind, and thermal performance.[4]

Durability of the MH Structure

HUD's research into durability issues focused on the causes and extent of degradation to the MH structure. Because an MH is designed to be moved at least once, potential for degradation exists as a result of transportation conditions. Further degradation is also possible during unit setup and takedown at the site. Thus the primary focus of durability research was on transportation impacts.

A factory-new MH was assumed to be "undegraded." Changes in the extent of structural stiffness (vertical and horizontal) and integrity of the unit were measured after transportation and setup. The researchers tested both single- and multisection MHs. Test data were reported for each section of a multisection MH. Tests involved transportation over roads of various conditions, in various weather conditions, and at various speeds. Each MH unit had several trips, thus several setups and takedowns.

Five parameters were identified to influence MH degradation. These parameters are in descending order of importance as determined by the research:

1. Effective torsional stiffness (resistance to horizontal forces or turns);
2. Road surface conditions;
3. MH in-transit speed;
4. Effective flexural stiffness (resistance to vertifical forces or twists); and
5. MH damping properties (resistance to bumps).

The first, effective torsional stiffness, is considered the key parameter (SwRI, 1979, Vol. 1).

Transportation, setup, and takedown do cause some degree of degradation, the amount increasing with additional distance traveled and with frequency of moves. Multisection MHs show more degradation than do single-section MHs primarily because only five rather than six sides are completely interconnected during transit. The most common evidence of degradation is separation at joint attachments—where walls adjoin the floor and ceiling. Other possible problems include misalignment of the sections of multisection units and a reduction in the holding power of fasteners, particularly in the roof-to-sidewall connections.

Researchers found that MH setup and takedown can cause more degradation than can transit. Degradation at this time results from the uneven raising and lowering of the MH unit. Failure to jack up both ends simultaneously can create severe vertical and/or horizontal stress. Since this stress can occur over an extended period of time, as compared to the relatively short-term stress of a turn or bump on a road, the possibility of damage is considerably higher.

Table 2–2 presents the amount of degradation due to transportation, setup, and takedown predicted for the two tested MHs, based on the experimental data collected. The table also presents a predicted degradation for the units constructed to standards proposed by the HUD researchers; the proportionate decrease in each case is substantial. For multisections it is quite dramatic and is attributable in large part to the research recommendation that temporary cross-bracing during transit be used in the open sections of the mating walls. Other recommendations included a maximum in-transit speed of 45 mph, choice of better roads, upgrading and/or increase in the number of certain fasteners, and changes in wall materials.

The research also attempted to assess the environmental and occupancy effects on the durability of MHs. As with the transportation element of the research, this effort met with considerable criticism of its methods, assumptions, and outcome. As a result HUD has undertaken additional data collection and analysis.

Durability analyses have also been completed for certain materials used in MHs. Strictly speaking, the use of a given material in an MH will have performance characteristics intrinsic to the material, rather than as a function of its use in an MH. However, certain use and design considerations may result from the necessary movement of MHs or from certain expected siting or environmental conditions.

Thus knowledge of the probable region of use of MH units built at a given factory may influence selection of structural adhesives. Research in this area, however, did yield the conclusion

Table 2–2 Predicted MH Degradation Due to Transportation, Setup, and Takedown under As-Tested and Proposed Standards

		Predicted Degradation (%)	
	Miles Traveled	*As-Tested*	*Proposed Standard*
Single-section MH	487	2.8	.70
	77	0.5	.13
	107	0.8	.20
	316	3.4	.85
	317	4.1	1.03
	256	4.9	1.23
	308	8.6	2.15
Multisection MH			
"Wet side"	315	19.7	4.82
	272	20.8	5.09
	273	23.5	5.71
	259	26.3	6.37
	275	32.0	7.65
"Dry side"	315	10.3	2.51
	171	7.0	1.71
	180	8.7	2.12
	247	14.4	3.51
	246	17.2	4.20

SOURCES: Southwest Research Institute. 1979. *Mobile Home Research: Transportation and Site Installation*, Vol. 4. Washington, D.C.: HUD.

Technology and Economics, 1980. *Economic Benefit-Cost and Risk Analysis of Results of Mobile Home Safety Research: Transportation Safety and Durability Analysis*. Washington, D.C.: HUD.

Note: Predictions assume 50 percent well-paved and 50 percent secondary roads.

that rational design and good quality control in the plant should be sufficient to guarantee the durability of adhesives for the desired useful life standard of 30 years[5] (Krueger and Sandberg, 1979).

Vulnerability of MHs to Fire

The perception that MHs are more vulnerable than other forms of single-family housing to fire, and their occupants more prone to injury and death due to these fires, was a major motivating factor in the passage by the Congress of the 1974 act. At the outset of HUD's research, available data indicated that although the fire

Table 2–3   Comparison of Fire Incidence and Fatality Rates between Site-Built and Manufactured Homes

	Fire Incidents per 100,000 Houses	*Fatalities per 100,000 Houses*	*Fatalities per Million Population*
Site-built homes (all)	534.5	4.20	13.5
Manufactured homes (all)	534.1	12.42	49.9
Manufactured homes (pre-1976)	563.1	14.10	56.6
Manufactured homes (1976–1978)	378.9	3.44	13.8

SOURCE: Gates, Howard. 1980. *Comparison of Fire Risk in Mobile Homes and Site-built Homes.* Arlington, Va.: Manufactured Housing Institute.

Note: Rates are based on National Fire Information Reporting Service data for 1978.

incidence rate was approximately the same for MHs and other housing forms, the injury and life hazard and the extent of property damage per incident were three to five times greater in MHs (Budnick and Klein, 1979).

Data on Causes of Fires. The available data on fires are of uneven quality, notably in terms of comparing age and type of structure involved. Current estimates suggest that between 12,000 and 20,000 MH fires are reported annually, which cause 400 to 450 deaths, 1,000 to 1,600 injuries, and $70 to $120 million in direct property loss (T&E, 1980c). Few studies attempt comparisons between MHs and site-built homes. One study, prepared for the Manufactured Housing Institute, confirms the general perception of equivalent rate of fires but higher frequency of fatality in MHs (Gates, 1980a). An interesting finding is the dramatic decrease in fire incidence and rate of fatalities in MHs built since the institution of the HUD Code (see Table 2–3). This drop in fatality rate concurs with a prediction made by the National Fire Data Center that the fatality rates for MHs and other single-family houses will be equivalent by the year 2000 (HUD, 1980, p. VI–1).

MHs have roughly the same cause distribution of fires as do one- and two-family homes (see Table 2–4). The one significant difference—the electrical distribution system—is the second most frequent cause of fires in MHs. This is probably attributable to the relatively prevalent use of aluminum wiring in MHs during the early 1970s. This wiring can create a fire hazard at switches and plugs. When aluminum wiring is used in combination with lauan

Table 2–4   Causes of Fires in MHs and One- and Two-Family Homes,
1978 (by percent)

Cause of Fire	One- and Two-Family Homes	Manufactured Homes
Heating	22	22
Cooking	15	13
Incendiary/suspicious	10	7
Smoking	7	6
Electrical distribution system	8	15
Appliances	7	7
Children	6	3
Other equipment	4	4
Exposure	3	3
Natural	1.3	1
Open flame	4	4
Other flame	2	0.5
Unknown	10	15

SOURCE: U.S. Fire Administration. 1980. *Highlights of Fire in the United States*, 2nd ed. Washington, D.C.: Federal Emergency Management Agency.

Note: Columns do not total 100 percent due to rounding.

plywood paneling, a frequently used interior wall finish with a relatively high-flame-spread classification (FSC), the potential for fire from this source increases considerably. (The HUD Code has eliminated the use of aluminum wiring.)

The voluntary standards provided for smoke detectors; the HUD Code made that provision mandatory. HUD's research has found that MHs with smoke detectors have 30 percent fewer fire deaths, 27 percent fewer injuries, and 10 percent less dollar loss (HUD, 1980, p. VI–2). The HUD Code also provides for range hoods over stoves and materials with low-flame-spread classification (maximum = 50) around stoves. Similarly, the HUD Code provides that furnace and water heater space be enclosed by walls, ceiling, and doors with a low-flame-spread classification (maximum = 25).

Flame-Spread Tests. Having provided for warning to occupants, for reducing ignition from electrical systems, and for containing fuel-fed fires at origin (stove, furnace, and water heater) through code provisions, much of HUD's research on fires has focused on the potential for growth and spread. About 25 percent of MH fires are confined to the ignited object, 11 percent stay in only a part of the room, 16 percent burn the entire room, and 48 percent burn more than the room of origin (HUD, 1980, p. VI–6). HUD's research looked especially at the contribution of room geometry and combustible finishes to rapid fire development.

Two general findings are particularly pertinent to MH fire safety: The first has to do with room geometry, the second with surface finishes. Single-section MHs frequently have a relatively long, narrow corridor, providing access to the two rear bedrooms and bathroom. Fire tests showed that an incidental fire entering such a corridor—rather than venting itself by burning up through the roof or out windows located along the corridor or burning through the partitions into adjacent areas—initially progressed directly down the length of the corridor and significantly limited occupant egress (Budnick and Klein, 1979, p. 10). This lateral flame movement is exacerbated by wall and ceiling finishes with a high FSC. In the corridor, as in other rooms, the rate of fire growth and spread, the severity of the fire, and the resulting conditions limiting life safety related directly to the thermophysical and fire properties of the wall and ceiling materials (Budnick and Klein, 1979, p. 11).

Building materials are given a FSC using a procedure approved by the American Society for Testing and Materials (ASTM). HUD's research tested various combinations of materials typically used for walls and ceilings in MHs: gypsum board, standard or specially treated lauan plywood, and ceiling tile. The tests were conducted in laboratory conditions to compare the combinations in terms of three major concerns:

1. Ignition time: How long it takes for walls and ceilings to ignite from the initially burning object.
2. Flashover: How long it takes for the fire to move to other rooms.
3. Effects on human response: How long it takes before the room is too hot, too smoky, has too much carbon monoxide (or too little oxygen) for people to behave normally in response to the fire.

Table 2–5 presents the results of tests on five combinations of wall and ceiling materials. For each test the initial burning of the interior was accomplished by the ignition of a 14-pound wood "crib" placed in a corner one inch from wall surfaces. The crib was constructed of 28 pieces of 2 by 2 hemlock fir, each 14 inches long and stacked in 2 rows of 2 and 6 rows of 4 sticks each. The

Table 2–5 Flame-Spread Test Results (time in minutes : seconds)

Material: Wall/Ceiling	Time to Wall Ignition	Time to Reach Ceiling	Time to Flashover	Time to 212°F	Time to Smoke Problem for Occupants	Time to Exceed Carbon Monoxide Maximum	Time to Exceed Oxygen Minimum
G/G	4:34	NR	NR	12:30	NR	NR	NR
LPC/G	3:06	3:48	5:14	3:47	3:48	NR	NR
LPS/T	3:34	3:54	4:56	4:10	4:15	NR	NR
LPS/G	3:36	4:22	5:33	4:33	4:54	5:31	NR
LPC/T	3:45	4:29	5:29	4:22	4:25	NR	NR

SOURCE: Southwest Research Institute. 1980. *Full-Scale Fire Tests on Specific Wall and Ceiling Materials of Mobile Home Modules.* Washington, D.C.: HUD.

Note: Times are given in minutes : seconds from start of test fire.

NR = Not Reached

Key to Wall/Ceiling Material	Flame Spread Classification
G = 5/16" gypsum board, printed finish	15
LPC = 5/32" lauan plywood, intumescent coated	70
LPS = 5/32" lauan plywood, standard finish	200
T = 1/2" cellulosic fiber ceiling tile	55

test module was a 12 by 8 foot room, with an 8-foot ceiling, built to simulate MH construction conditions (SwRI, 1980).

Vulnerability of MHs to Wind

High winds alone, as well as winds accompanying major storms such as hurricanes, can cause damage to homes and threaten the life and safety of residents. Because many MHs are not located on permanent foundations, they and their occupants have been especially vulnerable to problems caused by winds.[6] Beyond hazards to life and safety, four kinds of damage can result from wind and related storms:

1. Damage from flying objects;
2. Damage from movement on site;
3. Damage from water leaks;
4. Structural failure.

HUD-Established Wind Zones. Not all parts of the country have the same risk of high winds. Meteorologists have established gradients for the annual extreme fastest wind speed, with a 50-year mean recurrence interval. Based on these data HUD has established two wind zones, with design standards established to accommodate the annual 2 percent chance of the designated wind speed (Figure 2–11). "Standard" Wind Zone 1, with a 70 mph speed standard, requires design for horizontal wind loads not less than 15 psf and a net uplift load of not less than 9 psf. The "Hurricane Resistive" Wind Zone 2, inclusive of areas above the 70 mph standard, requires a design for horizontal wind loads not less than 25 psf and a net uplift load of not less than 24 psf. The country is divided into three zones for roof loads. Design in the north zone is for 40 psf, the middle zone for 30 psf, and the south zone for 20 psf (Figure 2–12).

HUD's research analyzed the frequency and severity of various sorts of problems resulting from wind and related storms. Unfortunately, data were not available to distinguish between wind resistance of MHs built before and after implementation of the HUD Code because post-1976 data were not available for the analysis. It is believed that MHs built to the HUD Code perform better under severe wind conditions although, as noted below, performance may be more a function of the system used to provide wind stabilization than of the structural system per se.

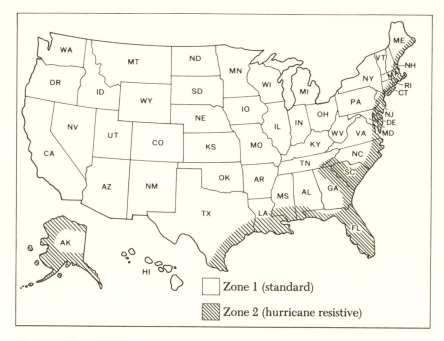

Figure 2–11 Wind Zones for MH Construction. *(Source: HUD Code.)*

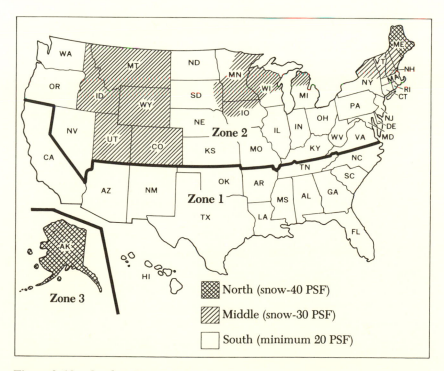

Figure 2–12 Outdoor Winter Design Temperature Zones and Roof Load Zones for MH Construction. *(Source: HUD Code.)*

Frequency and Severity of Wind Damage. The primary data used in the analysis of frequency and severity of MH wind problems were provided by a major MH insurer for the years 1970–1975 (see Table 2–6). For this period about 2 percent of MHs were damaged each year from high-speed winds. The proportion that suffered hurricane-related damage varied from .003 percent to .69 percent. The average cost of damage (in 1976 dollars) was $741 from high-speed winds and $2,617 from hurricane winds. From 1975 the National Weather Service reported 435 injuries and 21 deaths in MHs due to severe weather.[7]

About 25 percent of the damage was caused by flying objects, such as lawn furniture, garbage cans, and tree limbs; costs to repair averaged $200 to $400. Between 20 percent and 25 percent of damage occurred because MHs were not adequately secured to the ground. In these cases the MH shifted around on the site, resulting in twists and turns of the structure comparable to or even exceeding those experienced in transportation and setup. In some instances the MH turned over, causing damage averaging between $750 and $1500. Another 25 percent of damage was caused by water leaks that occurred during, but were not caused by, the storm. These leaks meant roof or wall repairs that averaged from $200 to $400. Because the final 25 percent to 30 percent of damage, structural failure caused by severe winds, is often not noticed soon after the storm, repair cost data were not available.

Wind Stabilization Systems. In addition to documenting frequency and severity of MH wind damage, HUD's research focused on approaches to provide adequate wind stabilization systems. MHs not on permanent foundations are particularly susceptible to both uplift and lateral wind force. Unless these units are somehow anchored to the ground, they can be blown upwards, sideways, or even over by strong winds. MHs not on permanent foundations can use wind stabilization systems to connect the unit to soil anchors. MHs that use adequate wind stabilization systems tend not to be blown around, over, or destroyed and suffer much less structural failure. The only damage they tend to experience is from flying objects (Kovacs and Yokel, 1979).

HUD's research concluded that most of the generally available wind stabilization systems will work. The factors influencing how well the system works include the following:

1. Matching the number and location of soil anchors to the MH unit and expected wind requirements;

Table 2–6 General Statistics on Damage to MHs and Personal Effects of the Occupants Due to High-Speed Winds, 1970–1975

Damage	1975	1974	1973	1972	1971	1970
Number of MHs in year round residential use (millions)	3.884	3.802	3.621	3.239	2.844	2.508
Number of MHs in Standard Wind Zone (millions)	3.884	3.802	3.621	3.239	2.844	2.508
Number of MHs in Hurricane Wind Zone	875,000	819,700	745,600	635,750	530,700	444,000
Number of MHs damaged in high winds	80,000	76,400	55,000	75,800	66,500	45,600
Number of MHs damaged by hurricanes	4,190	227	19	387	1,450	3,069
Average dollar loss in MHs damaged by high winds (1976 dollars)	$496	$620	$668	$991	$889	$828
Average dollar loss in MHs damaged by hurricanes (1976 dollars)	$1,273	$921	$90	$1,986	$846	$5,544

SOURCE: Adapted from Technology & Economics. 1980. *Economic Benefit-Cost and Risk Analysis of Results of Mobile Home Safety Research: Wind Safety Analysis*. Washington, D.C.: HUD.

2. Making certain the anchoring system selected is appropriate to soil conditions;
3. Installing the system properly, including "preloading" of the soil anchors.

There are three general types of soil anchor (see Figure 2–13). Some, such as the triangular, helix, and multihelix, are driven or turned directly into the soil. A second type, including the expanding plate and shaft, expanding rock, "X," and dead-man, are placed in excavated holes. A third type involves putting bolts or anchors in concrete footings or slabs. Two approaches are used to connect the unit to the soil anchor: (1) The near-tie connects each I-beam to its nearest anchor and (2) the far-tie crosses under the unit to connect to a far-side anchor.

The absence of clear descriptions and standards of soils and rocks makes it difficult to match anchoring systems to ground conditions. Moreover, soil strengths are subject to seasonal change, making this problem even more complex. Soil and rock composition analysis also varies in accuracy according to the test procedure, with the soil test probe regarded as the most acceptable (Kovacs and Yokel, 1979).

In addition to soil conditions, origin of the force causing pull-out is an important consideration for MH wind stabilization systems. Winds tend to create a stronger horizontal force, whereas

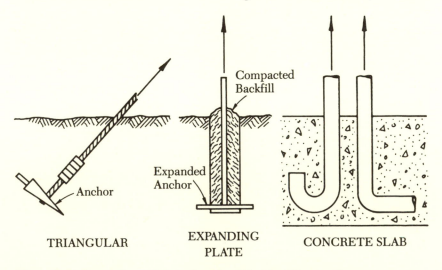

TRIANGULAR   EXPANDING   CONCRETE SLAB
                       PLATE

Figure 2–13 Examples of Soil Anchors for Wind Stabilization Systems.

floods cause vertical forces. Analysis has shown that the near-tie arrangement experiences lower vertical but greater horizontal force than does the far-tie arrangement. Thus conventional wind stabilization systems, characterized by anchors installed nearly vertical to the MH, may not be capable of resisting the horizontal force of hurricane winds without excessive displacement. The specific system used, therefore, must account for probable local conditions, with the number of diagonal ties predicated on wind load requirements, and the number of vertical ties based on flood load requirements.

Energy Considerations

The HUD Code identifies three climatic zones—warm, cold, and coldest—for which each MH is designed and constructed to withstand the winter temperatures (see Figure 2–12). HUD's Code sets threshold standards for thermal performance; for example, the practical effect for Zone 2 is R–19 insulation in the ceiling/roof and R–11 in the walls and floor. Zones 2 and 3 are required to have either insulated glass or exterior storm windows. HUD's Code further requires that each MH purchaser be provided with information about the thermal envelope of the purchased unit.

Thermal Envelope Performance. Research on thermal envelope performance showed that units performed within specified ranges. Although the code does not require it, vapor barriers are recommended to minimize moisture problems in walls. A related issue is the impact of foundation enclosures (or "skirting") on thermal performance. While such enclosures serve an important aesthetic function, they do not improve the performance of the thermal envelope per se, except to reduce the wind chill factor. Since too tight an installation creates water condensation problems in these enclosures, they must be ventilated.

Each MH built to the HUD Code has a heating certificate showing the heating capacity of its furnace in terms of the lowest outside temperature at which 70°F can be maintained inside the home. The code encourages energy efficiency by limiting chimney flue heat loss to 25 percent. MHs use various types of hot air furnace, including oil, natural and LP gas, and electric. Furnaces tested in HUD's research met performance standards.

Research found fairly uniform room air temperature distributions from room to room. However, wide temperature gradients were found from floor to ceiling and from room center to walls; rather significant rates of change were also found. Both factors were deemed by researchers as departures from "livability" criteria (SAI, 1979*a*, pp. 1–3). Researchers attributed these conditions in test units to duct and register location and thermostat location and/or calibration. Unit siting, especially for single-section units with their high length-to-width ratio, can also influence temperature gradients from center to outer parts of rooms.

HUD's standards required that each MH have a comfort cooling certificate. If the MH is equipped with a central air conditioning system, the certificate will provide information on the cooling capacity in Btu/hour and the maximum outdoor temperature at which 75°F can be maintained in the home. If the air distribution system is suitable to subsequent installation of central air conditioning, the certificate provides sizing information. The certificate will also indicate if the system cannot accommodate a central air conditioning system.

Like heating, the cooling load of a home depends on its location, structure, and occupants and is strongly influenced by the orientation of the home to the sun. Single-section MHs with large southerly exposures will experience significant "solar gain," with consequent heavy demands on the cooling system.

A research recommendation applicable to both heating and cooling concerns is the wrapping of under-floor ducts with R–4 insulation material to eliminate losses at this point.

A result of improved thermal performance in any structure is the reduction in the rate of air change. Thus what in one area is a benefit may result in a hazardous side effect in another. With reduced ventilation, certain contaminants, such as carbon monoxide, may remain within the home and reduce the air quality below a healthy level. HUD's research concluded that there is a more than adequate air change in MHs built to the HUD Code (SAI, 1979*b*). However, unique difficulties may result from one contaminant—formaldehyde.

Formaldehyde Contamination.   Formaldehyde is an industrial chemical used in the production of resins. Resin comprises about 10 percent of the weight of particleboard and plywood, which are used in much of the interior of MHs, particularly for paneling. These wood products can emit a formaldehyde vapor which, in sufficient quantities, may create health problems. Moreover, in sufficient dosages, formaldehyde can cause various health problems to the eyes, skin, and respiratory and digestive systems. The extent and seriousness of the formaldehyde problem is difficult to determine because people do not generally relate such symptoms to this possible cause and because knowledge is limited on dose-response relationships.

Not all MHs have the same potential for formaldehyde-caused health problems. Research to date has identified several possible reasons for this (Geomet, 1980):

1. *Age*: It appears that most formaldehyde vapors are emitted during the first year, and almost all by the fourth year after the MH is built.
2. *Space*: A relationship may exist between the volume of air space and the amount of wood products, with more air space constituting a lower formaldehyde vapor to air proportion.
3. *Production techniques*: Use of certain raw materials, resin ratios, additives, blending, pressing, and preparation techniques minimizes the potential for formaldehyde emissions.
4. *Occupant living habits*: More frequent change of air, either by chance (doors opened frequently) or intent (installation of air-to-air exchangers) reduces formaldehyde content of the interior air.

It is also possible to apply sealants to various wood surfaces in MHs with formaldehyde problems to reduce emissions.

HUD is conducting additional research on the frequency and severity of the problems, as well as working with the wood and MH industries on possible solutions. Pending outcomes of this work, two states (Minnesota and Wisconsin) have suspended plans to implement formaldehyde-related air quality standards for MHs.[8]

MH Quality: Code Comparisons

One mechanism to establish the quality of MHs is to compare them with other forms of single-family house construction. Because no research systematically compares such structures by actual performance, the alternative is to consider input evidence, namely construction codes.[9] A number of such comparisons exist. Four are found in the Appendix and compare the HUD Code with (1) the 1978 BOCA single-family-dwelling code; (2) the UBC

(1976), UPC (1976), and NEC (1978) codes for single-family dwellings; (3) the UBC modular code; and (4) the SBCC code. The first comparison was prepared by a state official, the other three by the engineering departments of two major MH manufacturers.

Each comparison identifies a category and then provides a summary statement of the pertinent requirements for each code. The BOCA/HUD Code comparison also determines whether the HUD Code requirement is the same as or more or less stringent than the BOCA Code stipulation. None provides any explicit conclusions about the quality of MHs, either intrinsically or in relation to the structures governed by the comparison code. Implicit in the presentation is the assertion of essential similarity, given the threshold premise of a construction standard.[10]

In that the purpose of construction codes is to provide reasonable protection to the public's health and safety while occupying the structures built to those codes, and given the assumption of responsibility of framers and certifiers of those codes, it seems reasonable to conclude that construction according to each of the codes yields houses of acceptable quality.[11]

Notes

1. Bernhardt (1980) contains several excellent chapters on MH production, including an analysis of cost and price structures.
2. My thanks to Ed Keiser of Burlington Homes for giving Bill Allan and me full run of the plant to obtain most of these photos.
3. HUD defines an MH as ". . . a structure, transportable in one or more sections, which is eight body feet or more in width and is thirty-two body feet or more in length, and which is built on a permanent chassis, and designed to be used as a dwelling with or without permanent foundation, when connected to the required utilities, and includes the plumbing, heating, air-conditioning, and electrical systems contained therein."
4. I am especially appreciative of the assistance of Jim McCollom who provided and helped interpret HUD's MH research.
5. Studies of plumbing and electrical systems in MHs had not been released as of this writing.
6. MHs on permanent foundations tend to lose their identity as MHs, especially in various data collection efforts. When permanently sited, MHs are often reported with other single-family detached homes. Consequently, little is known about the performance of these MH units in the face of wind and storms. It is important to remember that the research reported here covers only those MHs not permanently sited.

7. This is very likely an underestimation due to reporting procedures. See T&E, 1980b, pp. 43–45.

8. Georgia-Pacific announced in early 1981 voluntary product standards effectively limiting formaldehyde emissions to an ambient air level of less than 0.50 parts per million (*Merchandiser*, 1981b).

9. A Department of Defense proposal to compare 200 MHs and 254 site-built houses at its Fort Irwin, California, Army National Training Center may provide useful direct comparison data. The proposal received congressional authorization in spring 1981.

10. Another comparison (Gates, 1980*b*) prepared for the Manufactured Housing Institute considers the HUD Code and HUD's Minimum Property Standards for financing eligibility under its Title II loan programs of site-built single-family dwellings. This comparison concludes that only "insignificant differences in required structural performance" exist between the two standards. These differences are not considered consequential to the minimum quality of the house as established by the standard, but to the differences in orientation (factory- versus site-built).

11. However, in the absence of specific and objective data and analysis of housing built to each code, the instinct to scholarly skepticism remains. What is unfortunate is that the research on housing built to HUD's MH Code was conducted in a vacuum and that research on housing performance in general seems to proceed primarily on a "management-by-exception" basis—that is, research considers only what fails. Thus we are unable to positively conclude anything about what does not fail. However, if it is acceptable to make public policy on the basis that "if it does not fail it is acceptable," one would reasonably conclude that among the forms of acceptable single-family detached dwellings are those built to the HUD MH Code as well as those built to the various model codes (BOCA, UBC, etc.), whether built on-site or in a factory.

Chapter 3

MH DISTRIBUTION

The off-site construction of MHs has led to an industry organization that differs substantially from that for site-built housing. Historically, the primary participants in the MH industry have been manufacturers, transporters, and dealers. The industry structure that relied on these three primary participants, while still dominant, is in the process of changing. This chapter discusses the traditional MH distribution system, then notes current and possible changes.

The Traditional Distribution System

The traditional distribution system has three primary components —manufacturers, dealers, and transporters—with a unique approach to financing of industry activities and home purchase.

MH Manufacturers

Approximately 180 companies produce MHs in about 420 plants located throughout the country (MHI, 1981a). Most large companies have plants located in several parts of the United States, many having 10 or more plants. However, the more frequent situation is a single plant that includes the firm's headquarters staff. Based on 1979 data, the top 30 manufacturers (in dollar volume) account for over three fourths of all production (see Table 3–1). Most MH manufacturers build homes only to the HUD Code, although some build other forms of manufactured housing to state codes. A very few also construct site-built hous-

Table 3–1   Top MH Builders, 1979

Rank	Builder	MH Units	Volume* ($ million)
1	Guerdon Industries (City Investing)	14,829	542.0**
2	Kaufman and Broad	6,670	358.3**
3	Skyline Corp.	25,997	327.4
4	Fleetwood Enterprises	20,346	288.8**
5	Redman Industries	14,542	204.9
6	The Commodore Corp.	14,164	177.8
7	Wick Building Systems	7,832	172.8**
8	Champion Home Builders	15,420	152.6
9	Schult Homes (Inland Steel)	7,731	134.9**
10	Liberty Homes	12,783	109.2
11	Shelter Resources Corp.	6,341	101.8
12	Golden West Homes	3,584	84.6
13	Fairmont Homes	7,000	80.0
14	Brigadier Industry Corp.	7,743	74.5
15	Silvercrest Industries	3,000	71.7
16	Zimmer Homes Corp.	5,026	68.2
17	Tidwell Industries	5,431	62.0
18	Fuqua Homes	2,712	53.0
19	Marlette Homes	2,480	47.0
20	Oakwood Homes	3,299	44.4
21	Moduline International	3,279	40.8
22	Conchemco Homes Group	2,955	37.3
23	Vintage Enterprises	2,718	35.1
24	Horton Homes	3,856	31.2
25	Nobility Homes	2,813	30.1
26	Chief Industries	1,813	27.6
27	Connor Homes	3,214	25.8
28	DMH, Co.	1,860	25.0
29	Manufactured Housing Management Corp.	1,740	24.9
30	Mobile Home Industries	1,852	24.8
	Total	212,835	3,458.5
	Total 1979 MH Shipment	276,880	
	Top MH Builders % of Total 76.9%		

SOURCE: *Automation in Housing and Systems Building News,* August 1980.

* Volume is for all forms of housing constructed.
** Indicates that the company builds more than MHs.

Table 3–2 Comparison of MH Shipments and Sales of Single-Family Site-Built Houses, All Prices, 1975–1980

	1975	1976	1977	1978	1979	1980
Site-Built Houses						
Houses sold	550,000	647,000	820,000	817,000	709,000	531,000
Percentage of total	72	72	76	75	72	71
MHs						
Houses shipped	212,690	246,120	265,145	274,901	276,121	221,000
Percentage of total	28	28	24	25	28	29
Total	762,690	893,120	1,085,145	1,091,901	985,121	752,000

SOURCE: Manufactured Housing Institute. 1981. *Quick Facts about the Manufactured Housing Industry.*

ing, but these cases typically involve conglomerates, with the MH manufacturer being an independent subsidiary of a larger corporation.

MH manufacturers produce a surprisingly large number and proportion of annual additions to the housing stock. Table 3–2 presents information on single-family housing construction for the period 1975–1980, in which MHs accounted for roughly one quarter of new units. Similarly, MH firms listed in the top 100 volume builders account for over one half of all units, but for less than one third of dollar volume (see Table 3–3). The lower dollar volume share is attributable in part to lower square foot costs of MHs, to inclusion of some multifamily units in the total, and to

Table 3–3 MH and Non-MH Production by Top 100 Firms, by Units and Dollar Volume, 1979

	Units		Dollar Volume	
	Number	Percent	$ million	Percent
Non-MH	173,339	44.9	8,573.7	71.3
MH	212,835	55.1	3,458.5	28.7
Total	386,174	100.0	12,032.2	100.0

SOURCE: *Automation in Housing and Systems Building News.* August 1980.

Note: Data eliminates one firm that produced exclusively for the foreign market. Survey included (1) production builders, (2) panelized home builders, (3) modular home builders, and (4) MH builders. Some builders produced multi- as well as single-family housing.

Table 3–4   Manufactured Home Shipments and Estimated Sales Volume, 1950–1980

Year	Shipments	Estimated Retail Sales (in $ millions)
1980	221,097	$4,245
1979	276,121	4,860
1978	274,901	4,378
1977	265,145	3,765
1976	246,120	3,136
1975	212,690	2,432
1974	329,300	3,213
1973	566,920	4,406
1972	575,940	4,002
1971	496,570	3,297
1970	401,190	2,451
1969	412,690	2,496
1968	317,950	1,907
1967	240,360	1,370
1966	217,300	1,238
1965	216,470	1,212
1964	191,320	1,071
1963	150,840	862
1962	118,000	661
1961	90,200	505
1960	103,700	518
1959	120,500	602
1958	102,000	510
1957	119,300	596
1956	124,330	622
1955	111,900	462
1954	76,000	325
1953	76,900	322
1952	83,000	320
1951	67,300	248
1950	63,100	216

SOURCE: Manufactured Housing Institute. 1981. *Quick Facts about the Manufactured Housing Industry.*

Note: Prior to 1950, production varied from 1,300 in 1930 upward to 46,200 in 1949.

certain non-MH builders constructing a relatively large number of units specifically for the upper end of the shelter market, thus raising significantly the average dollar volume for non-MH builders.

Shipments of MH units by manufacturers fluctuate year to year, responding to a variety of economic and market conditions. Annual shipments have not been fewer than 200,000 annually since 1964, with the peak production of over 575,000 units occurring in 1972. Table 3–4 presents annual shipments and estimated retail sales from 1950 to 1980.

MH Dealers

MHs are sold to consumers through a system of retail dealers, which total approximately 10,000 in the United States. In its traditional form this system is similar to that serving the automobile industry. A dealer firm will sell homes built by one or more manufacturers. Homes are displayed for buyer inspection on dealer sales lots. Many dealers simply present an array of MHs in temporary set-up condition, while other dealers arrange a more permanent setup of display units, replicating park or individual site conditions.

Although the majority of dealers operate only a single sales lot, there is a trend to "chain" operation, with nearly 10 percent of dealers in 1977 operating five or more lots (Bernhardt, 1980, p. 173). Outlets are located in commercial zones and often have conspicuous site advertising. About one half of dealers sell MHs only, with the remainder selling recreation vehicles and travel trailers as well (Bernhardt, 1980, p. 157).

Most sales lots also serve as the site for the dealer's service operation. Depending on the size of the dealership, the service operation will include some or all of the following: service and repair, accessories and parts stock and sales, interior decoration, home maintenance, and transportation and setup. Similarly, the sales operation may have degrees of specialization, depending on the size of the dealership.

One of the basic services provided by dealers is financing. Since financing of MH purchases will be described in greater detail later in this chapter and in Chapter 4, it is sufficient for current purposes to note that the financing services traditionally provided again parallel those in the auto industry—namely, facilitating consumer installment loans with banks or finance companies. (The financing of distribution will be described in a later section of this chapter.)

In addition to sales of MHs, many dealers are involved in MH park development and operation. Providing the site as well as the unit enhances the possibility of sales and increases the related profit. Many parks of an earlier vintage were located adjacent to the sales lot, with either the same commercial zoning or a special MH park zone classification. Operating MH parks also provides a means for dealers to be involved in sales of existing MH units.

MH Transporters

The connection between site of manufacture and site of occupancy is made by the transporter. Transporters move MH units from manufacturer to dealer or directly from manufacturer to the purchaser's site. They also move units from dealers to home sites and, in cases of subsequent moves, from site to site. Depending on the transporter and conditions of transport, the service may include trip preparation and setup.

Transporters include those with ICC authorization for interstate routes and those that transport primarily intrastate. Dealers may also be in the transportation business, providing the service only for their own customers or also on a fee basis for manufacturers, other dealers, or MH owners.

Approximately 70 percent of all hauling is from the manufacturer to the dealer, with the remaining amount accounted for by the shorter distances of dealer to site and site to site movement. The manufacturer-to-dealer hauling is done primarily by transporters with ICC authorization. Although there are approximately twenty nationwide firms, it is estimated that three of the companies account for about 85 percent of the revenues (Bernhardt, 1980, p. 292).

Manufacturers use transporters for long hauls because of the efficiencies involved. Nationwide firms have multiple terminals to avoid the costs of empty return trips. Furthermore, the nationwide firms are familiar with regulations and regulators on a state-by-state basis. However, manufacturers do maintain their own transportation fleets for short-distance, intrastate trips.

As compared with manufacturers, dealers do much of their own transportation—the distances involved are shorter, and regular repetition of routes afford dealers (and localized transporters) a competitive advantage in terms of highly specific knowledge of regulation and regulators for small areas. Dealers use transporters on a local basis when sales exceed their own delivery and setup capacity.

Distribution Financing

Financing for MH manufacturers is on a basis similar to other manufacturing corporations. Unlike the early years of the MH industry, which were characterized by ease of entry and out-of-pocket capitalization, contemporary MH corporate operations are notable for differentiation of task and responsibility and systematic application of modern business management methods. Many of the largest firms in the industry trade stock publicly. Even the smaller firms produce sufficient units to yield large-scale annual revenues. The size of initial investment in plant and material required for industry competitiveness and the accompanying need for management skill combine to limit ease of entry. This corporate dimension of MH manufacturing, however, does provide for more secure and favorable financing, internal planning, research and development, and the ability to benefit from economies of scale.

Financing of MH dealer activities has many unique attributes, deriving in large part from the tradition of treating MH sales very much like other high-cost manufactured personal goods. Because the traditional method of financing dealer activities has tied dealer purchase of MH inventory to ultimate occupant financing of unit purchase, the two will be treated together in the following paragraphs.[1]

Like the auto dealer, the MH dealer requires financing for both inventory and buyers. Because MHs are legally defined as personal property, the typical financing arrangement for the buyer has been a relatively short-term installment loan.[2] Lenders often provide inventory financing (referred to in the MH industry as "floor planning") to a dealer to obtain preferred access to a dealer's retail financing business. These accounts are attractive to lenders because of the higher interest rates and shorter maturities. Lenders may also condition construction loans or long-term park development mortgages with dealers on access to retail financing, a practice similar to takeout mortgage financing in subdivisions.

Inventory financing arrangements are as might be expected, with cash advanced for wholesale purchases against expectations of revenues from sales and services. The terms of the financing may vary depending on the extent of involvement of the lender in the retail accounts of the dealer.

By comparison the retail financing arrangements involve considerable interdependencies, with dealers doing credit initiation and review and lenders sharing certain income from the loan in return for the dealer's review services and/or risk sharing by guaranteeing some or all of the note. Dealer participation in note guarantee has had the effect of easing buyer access to MH financing. Because lenders do not carry as high a risk for default, they tend not to scrutinize the loan application as closely. Dealers, anxious to make sales, have similar incentive to make the financing available. The results from this somewhat easier financing are higher interest rates on notes, thus reflecting the perception of a potential for higher loss experience.

The permanent lender (a finance company, bank, or thrift institution) may make certain requirements to secure his risk. Since not all states require titling (those that do typically title using motor vehicle procedures, as discussed in Chapter 5), the permanent lender may require that the certificate of origin be filed with the title document, which will also record the lien against the MH unit (if it serves as the note's security). Typically, the financing arrangements will also be summarized on a uniform commercial code (UCC) form and filed with the appropriate public office.

Dealer financing is facilitated in many instances by service companies. These companies serve a brokerage role, drawing together and providing services to lenders, dealers, manufacturers, and insurance companies. They may be subsidiaries or departments of lenders and therefore provide lending themselves. They provide credit review and home appraisals, loan administration, and note insurance, and they assist in FHA and VA loans, as well as those solely in the private market.

The Changing Distribution System

The system that provides for distribution of this housing form is evidencing current and potential changes. These changes relate to manufacturers, dealers, finance, and the organizations that serve to focus and coordinate industry activities.

National Organizations

The nature and focus of national organizations of the MH industry have changed as the role of this housing form in the shelter industry has begun to shift.

The Manufactured Housing Institute. The largest of the organizations, the Manufactured Housing Institute (MHI), was established in 1936 as the Mobile Homes Manufacturers Association. Many of its early functions were social and were supplemented by serving as a means to facilitate contact among manufacturers and suppliers. During the 1950s a major activity was encouraging the development of MH parks as a unique spatial and legal form of housing development. Many of its 1960s activities were aimed at issues of product quality, utilizing the voluntary standards process to develop and gain acceptance for an industrywide construction and safety code.

When Congress mandated a single, preemptive code in 1974, MHI shifted its orientation toward public and governmental relations. Indicative of its efforts to promote acceptance of MHs by both consumers and public officials is its sponsorship in the spring of 1980 of a "House-on-the-Hill" program, for which MHs were placed on the Mall in Washington, with invitations to visit issued to the Congress, congressional staff, and federal agencies. A shift toward a slightly more educational orientation is indicated by the addition of a one-day "retailers" seminar to the annual nationally oriented MH show sponsored by MHI. The 1981 seminar, for example, focused on land development, with presentations on marketing, site development and finance.

The Western Manufactured Housing Institute. Indicative of the conflicting views on the future of the MH industry is the late 1970s split of the western wing of the MHI to form the Western Manufactured Housing Institute (WMHI). Based in California, and working primarily with the 13 western states, WMHI actively seeks market expansion and a movement of MHs into more traditional housing market areas. WMHI has supported efforts to change legal definitions and the tax status of MHs to conform with other forms of real property, advanced improvements in state and local development controls, and has promoted the development of MH communities and subdivisions.

These emphases have led to a focus on finance issues. Carrying on an activity begun while still a part of MHI, WMHI sponsors a national congress on manufactured housing finance, as well as an annual MH show. The organization has also supported, along with several of its member manufacturers and state associations, the formation and work of an ad hoc Coordinating Council on MH Finance. The Council works on issues relating to federal financing programs and federal regulation of MH financing by lending institutions.

The National Manufactured Housing Federation. A third organization, the National Manufactured Housing Federation (NMHF), was formed in 1977 to serve as a unified national voice for dealers, park owners, and developers. Serving as a coordinating mechanism for the various state and regional MH associations, whose constituencies are the dealer-park owner-developer segment of the MH industry, the NMHF works with the Congress and regulatory agencies on legislative and administrative issues of interest. It made a comprehensive set of proposals to the Congress relative to MHs in the 1981 Housing Bill, many of which were incorporated in the final bill.

Manufacturers

Within the parameters of traditional distribution from manufacturer through distributor to consumer, manufacturers are showing increased sophistication in assessing market preferences and promoting market demand. Whereas market preferences were once determined by a relatively seat-of-the-pants method—involving some combination of sales force field reports, anecdotes collected at MH shows, and dealer order trends—current marketing involves use of market research firms, computer-assisted analysis of order patterns, and direct analysis of consumer response through buyer surveys.

Larger firms are building sizable marketing departments to do direct marketing (print or visual media) on a regional and national basis and to provide various forms of marketing support for dealers. In addition to sales guides and training programs, firms provide (typically in some form of cost-sharing basis) print ads, direct mail pieces, radio and TV commercials, and a host of printed promotional material for use in direct sales efforts.

A second emerging development involves a move outside the parameters of the manufacturer-dealer connection. Some manufacturers are becoming involved in direct housing development, with such efforts typically undertaken as a joint venture with a local developer of existing reputation.[3] While still small, this trend could indicate either a movement away from reliance on dealers or a means to expand the manufacturer's market beyond that currently tapped by dealer activities. Since these housing developments tend to use multisection MHs and involve permanent foundations, thus entailing sale of both the land and unit, the latter outcome (namely new markets) is the more likely.

Dealers

Like manufacturers, dealers are exhibiting two shifts in distribution activity, one essentially in keeping with traditional patterns, and one a major change.

Traditional Dealer Shifts. The shift that keeps dealers within traditional patterns involves increasing activity with existing rather than new MHs. With the total number of MH units in the housing stock having doubled during the past decade, and with the quality of that stock having significantly improved, the market is solid and growing in sales of existing MH units. In situations where the unit is in a park owned and/or operated by the dealer, the sales brokerage function is obvious and the market readily captured (*Merchandiser*, February 1981). Dealers are also involved in sales of units in nonpark settings. In situations where these units are not affixed (and therefore still classified as personal property) the brokerage activity is not governed by a license requirement. However, when the unit is sited on owned land (and definitely if is it affixed and is classified as real property) brokerage license requirements apply. Increasingly, therefore, dealers are becoming licensed real estate brokers and in some cases becoming involved in sales of other forms of real estate as well. Similarly, real estate agents involved in sales of other forms of housing are becoming involved in sales of MHs, both in and out of MH parks (*Merchandiser*, September 1980).

An activity relating to the size and age of MH stock is the increasing involvement in what might be called the MH improvement and rehabilitation business. Although the areas of these activities do not differ from other housing forms (roofing, exterior walls, plumbing, heating, electrical systems, and so on), the nature of MH construction (especially of pre-HUD Code stock) is sufficiently unique as to require specific experience (if not skills). Recent trade journal and magazine articles suggest that among the major rehabilitation activities are energy retrofitting and exterior rehab/siding.

Subdivision Development. A major shift in dealer activities has been the involvement in subdivision development. Rather than selling units for placement in a park or on land already arranged for (on a lease or purchase basis) by the MH buyer, the dealer is becoming involved in direct development. While in some cases the development may be a horizontal condominium using MHs, and therefore providing potential management income, most developments are of the traditional subdivision form. Rather than selling the units at a sales lot, the developer locates one or more units at the development site as models to be sold on completion of the development.

Since the subdivision involves the sale of permanently affixed MH units (therefore real property), the financial arrangements between dealers and lenders take on a different form. Indeed the source of financing may be from a different lender altogether, or at least from a different department of the lending institution. However, while these elements are new to the dealer, they are characteristic routines of financing real estate development and sales for the lending institutions. Again, a secondary consequence of the movement of dealers into subdivision development has been the awakening interest of existing developers to use MHs in their developments.

Financing

Changes in MH financing can be summarized as "more like conventional real estate financing." That is, lenders are placing mortgages with longer terms and lower rates on real property they consider will appreciate in value. (The consumer involvement dimensions of financing will be discussed in Chapter 4.) The overall trends in nature and availability of financing as it impacts the distribution system will be summarized here.

Three factors combine to prompt changes in financing: size, cost, and location. MHs are larger, costlier, and increasingly are located on the unit owner's land. Table 3–5 presents cost and size information for the period 1973–1980. The size increase is primarily due to the proportionate increase of multisection MHs, which constituted about one third of all 1980 shipments, up from one tenth in 1970. Multisection MHs in particular tend to be sited on

Table 3–5 Cost and Size of Manufactured Homes, 1973–1980

Year	Average Sale Price*	Cost per Square Foot	Average Square Footage
1973	$ 7,770	$ 8.81*	882
1974	9,760	10.73*	910
1975	11,440	12.02*	952
1976	12,750	13.20*	966
1977	14,200	14.20*	1,000
1978	15,925	15.77	1,010
1979	17,700	16.86	1,050
1980	18,500	17.80	1,050

SOURCE: Manufactured Housing Institute. 1981. *Quick Facts about the Manufactured Housing Industry.*

* Includes furniture, draperies, carpeting, and appliances, but excludes transportation, land, and other applicable site preparation and set-up charges.

unit owner's land and have an appearance similar to other forms of single-family detached housing of this size. These units especially have attracted new forms of financing to the MH industry.

From 1976 to the end of 1980, the total value of MH retail paper outstanding increased from $14.2 billion to $17.4 billion. In 1980 the distribution of this paper by lending institution type was as follows: banks, 59.9 percent; finance companies, 21.6 percent; savings and loan associations, 15.8 percent; federal credit unions, 2.7 percent. (See Table 3–6.) Bank and credit union proportions

Table 3–6 MH Retail Paper Outstanding (in $ millions), by Type of Institution, 1976–1980

Year	All Banks	All Finance Companies	All S&Ls	All Federal Credit Unions
1976	8,233 (58.1%)	3,277 (23.1%)	2,360 (16.7%)	300 (2.0%)
1977	8,862 (59.8%)	3,109 (21.0%)	2,538 (17.1%)	300 (2.0%)
1978	9,553 (59.5%)	3,152 (19.6%)	2,848 (17.8%)	489 (3.0%)
1979	9,991 (57.4%)	3,390 (19.5%)	3,516 (20.2%)	512 (2.9%)
1980	10,376 (59.9%)	3,745 (21.6%)	2,737 (15.8%)	469 (2.7%)

SOURCE: Manufactured Housing Institute. 1980, 1981. *Manufactured Homes Financing.*

Table 3–7 Value of MH Retail Paper Outstanding, 1975–1980

	1975	1976	1977	1978	1979	1980
Banks						
Reporting institutions	321	315	307	309	285	277
Dollar value	2,297,150,000	2,258,628,000	2,045,515,000	3,316,223,000	3,683,167,000	3,571,731,000
Average account value	7,949	8,963	10,279	11,978	12,748	13,091
Accounts outstanding	288,685	251,861	199,431	276,851	288,920	272,848
Finance Companies						
Reporting institutions	34	40	29	22	28	28
Dollar value	2,624,485,000	3,254,333,000	3,474,297,000	3,893,833,000	5,185,802,000	6,898,131,000
Average account value	7,190	9,245	9,143	12,329	14,561	15,581
Accounts outstanding	364,801	351,545	379,971	315,817	356,139	442,716
Savings and Loan Associations						
Reporting institutions	64	94	89	75	76	82
Dollar value	446,921,000	806,947,000	1,093,540,000	1,020,615,000	1,216,283,000	1,443,801,000
Average account value	12,079	13,229	13,018	14,072	15,159	15,530
Accounts outstanding	37,109	60,662	83,546	72,527	80,235	92,967
Total, All Reporting Institutions						
Reporting institutions	419	449	425	406	389	387
Dollar value	5,368,556,760	6,319,908,000	6,613,352,000	8,230,671,000	10,085,252,000	11,913,663,000
Average account value	7,769	9,518	9,975	12,373	13,905	14,735
Accounts outstanding	690,595	664,068	662,948	665,195	725,294	808,531

SOURCE: Manufactured Housing Institute. 1980, 1981. *Manufactured Homes Financing.*

held relatively constant during this period, whereas S&Ls increased from 16.7 percent in 1976 to 20.2 percent in 1979, then dropped dramatically to 15.8 percent in 1980. Finance companies decreased from 23.1 percent in 1976 to 19.5 percent in 1979, then increased to 21.6 percent in 1980 (MHI, 1980, 1981b). A summary of financing volume trends based on MHI's annual survey of lenders is presented in Table 3–7.

One reason for the 1979 increase in S&L activity in MH financing was the liberalization that year by the Federal Home Loan Bank Board of the terms and conditions for MH lending. These changes permitted S&Ls to devote up to 20 percent of their assets to MH loans, more than twice the amount previously permitted; terms and maturities were also liberalized. The ability to pool FHA and VA insured loans for sale to GNMA also attracts traditional lender participation. Perhaps the final reason for S&L activity is that the form and price of MHs allows them to continue to serve their traditional home-buying market. S&L participation, however, depends on their ability to attract funds. The precipitous decline in S&L activity in 1980 indicates their more general difficulty in the money market.

Related to the increased participation in MH financing by traditional participants in the shelter loan market is a trend toward decreased participation by dealers in loan origination activities and proceeds. Inventory financing and the financing of sales are increasingly done by different institutions. Those with more traditional shelter market experience have moved to direct loans, with longer maturities and use of simple rather than add-on methods of computing interest. For reasons of both tradition and the size of the note, these lenders are also doing borrower qualifications directly, and by more conventional real estate based methods.

A factor related to increased lender interest in MH financing is the acceptable level and relative stability in account delinquencies and repossessions. This factor was of particular concern because the early 1970s were characterized by an extremely high rate of delinquencies and repossessions, which significantly undermined investor confidence. Table 3–8 presents data from MHI's finance survey on installment delinquencies from 1975 to 1980, which show a decrease in proportion of delinquencies. Information from the same source on repossessions during 1977 to 1980 is presented in Table 3–9; again the proportion has decreased. It should be noted that these data cover MHs financed primarily on a personal-

Table 3–8 MH Installment Loan Delinquencies, 1975–1980

	1975	%	1976	%	1977	%	1978	%	1979	%	1980	%
Banks												
Reporting institutions	310		310		296		301		260		257	
Accounts outstanding	283,513	100.0	245,338	100.0	197,142	100.0	256,082	100.0	242,427	100.0	258,400	100.0
Accounts delinquent	10,376	3.7	8,478	3.4	8,124	4.1	11,268	4.4	9,091	3.7	7,799	3.0
30–59 days	6,844	2.4	5,776	2.4	5,521	2.8	8,191	3.2	6,545	2.7	5,442	2.1
60–89 days	2,015	0.7	1,656	0.7	1,479	0.8	2,074	0.8	1,489	0.6	1,424	0.6
90 days plus	1,517	0.5	1,046	0.4	1,124	0.6	1,003	0.4	1,057	0.4	933	0.4
Finance companies												
Reporting institutions	33		40		29		22		22		26	
Accounts outstanding	361,301	100.0	351,545	100.0	379,971	100.0	315,817	100.0	336,939	100.0	436,127	100.0
Accounts delinquent	20,311	5.6	15,466	4.4	10,670	2.8	11,084	3.5	10,231	3.0	13,007	3.0
30–59 days	11,253	3.1	8,756	2.5	5,159	1.4	6,040	1.9	5,478	1.6	8,210	1.9
60–89 days	5,346	1.5	2,742	0.8	3,354	0.9	2,630	0.8	2,077	0.6	2,298	0.5
90 days plus	3,712	1.0	3,968	1.1	2,157	0.6	2,414	0.8	2,676	0.8	2,499	0.6
Savings and Loan Associations												
Reporting institutions	64		92		86		73		73		78	
Accounts outstanding	37,109	100.0	59,247	100.0	80,400	100.0	70,409	100.0	71,018	100.0	89,047	100.0
Accounts delinquent	1,758	4.7	2,544	4.3	3,413	4.2	2,439	3.5	3,106	4.4	3,038	3.4
30–59 days	1,023	2.8	1,528	2.6	2,224	2.8	1,558	2.2	1,988	2.8	2,003	2.2
60–89 days	340	0.9	510	0.9	667	0.8	505	0.7	606	0.9	514	0.6
90 days plus	395	1.0	506	0.9	522	0.6	373	0.5	512	0.7	521	0.6
Total, All Reporting Institutions												
Reporting institutions	407		442		411		396		355		361	
Accounts outstanding	681,923	100.0	656,130	100.0	657,513	100.0	642,308	100.0	650,384	100.0	783,574	100.0
Accounts delinquent	32,445	4.8	26,488	4.0	22,207	3.4	24,791	3.9	22,428	3.4	23,844	3.0
30–59 days	19,120	2.8	16,060	2.4	12,904	2.0	15,789	2.5	14,011	2.2	15,655	2.0
60–89 days	7,701	1.1	4,908	0.7	5,500	0.8	5,209	0.8	4,172	0.6	4,236	0.5
90 days plus	5,624	0.8	5,520	0.8	3,803	0.6	3,793	0.6	4,245	0.7	3,953	0.5

SOURCE: Manufactured Housing Institute. 1980, 1981. *Manufactured Homes Financing.*

Table 3–9 **Repossessions in Total MH Installment Accounts Outstanding, 1977–1980**

	1977	1978	1979	1980
Banks				
Number reporting	296	301	260	257
Accounts outstanding	197,142	256,082	242,427	258,400
Repossessions	1,368	1,367	1,120	1,223
Percentage	0.7	0.5	0.5	0.5
Finance Companies				
Number reporting	29	22	22	26
Accounts outstanding	379,971	315,817	336,939	436,127
Repossessions	2,477	2,131	1,950	2,497
Percentage	0.7	0.7	0.6	0.6
Savings & Loan Associations				
Number reporting	86	73	73	78
Accounts outstanding	80,400	70,409	71,018	89,047
Repossessions	592	588	469	563
Percentage	0.7	0.8	0.7	0.6
Totals, All Reporting Institutions				
Number reporting	411	396	355	361
Accounts outstanding	657,513	642,308	650,384	783,574
Repossessions	4,437	4,086	3,539	4,283
Percentage	0.7	0.6	0.5	0.5

SOURCE: Manufactured Housing Institute. 1980, 1981. *Manufactured Homes Financing.*

property basis. Lending institutions do not tend to differentiate in data reporting real property SFD loans by structural type. Thus the complete picture on borrower behavior on all forms of MH loans cannot be portrayed.

Notes

1. A very able summary of dealer financing, as well as issues surrounding it is contained in New Jersey Legislative Study Commission, pp. 169–253.
2. The definition of "short-term" here is relative to home mortgage maturities. For example, in the mid-1970s, when home mortgages were 20 to 25 years, MH chattel mortgages were 7 to 13 years to maturity.
3. It should be noted that some few manufacturers have done direct sales to consumers for some time. These sales offices, however, have functioned in most respects like dealerships and thus do not constitute a significant separate category in terms of industry structure.

Chapter 4

MARKET ISSUES

The previous two chapters have dealt with how MHs are built, the regulatory environment within which construction occurs, assessments of the construction quality and safety of MHs, and traditional and emerging ways in which MHs reach their markets. This chapter deals with topics directly related to MH housing markets, including distribution and mix of MH types nationally; who buys, rents, and lives in MHs; cost, value, and financing; and a variety of consumer affairs and perception issues.

Characteristics and Location of MH Residents

MHs can be located on owned or rented land and can be grouped or individually sited. The development of the MH industry included the creation of a unique form of housing development, the MH park, which accounts for the location of about one half of all MH units. In an MH park all the units are of one structural type—MH. The units are typically owned by the occupant. However, the land and related improvements—streets, infrastructure, recreational buildings, and so on—are owned by someone else, to whom residents pay a monthly fee to cover lot rental, services and facilities, real estate taxes, and any other unique provisions of the park. Usually the owner is an individual proprietor or a corporation with an on-site manager. A recent, though not yet large, trend involves condominium or cooperative corporation park ownership by the residents. Another relatively recent trend (noted in Chapter 3) is the use of MHs in subdivision development, with the unit and land sold as a package.

Unfortunately, the data for profiling MH residents are severely limited in terms of availability, uniformity of definition, inclusiveness, and coverage of time. Data from the Census, and the related Annual Housing Survey (AHS), usually the most reliable source for comprehensive information on housing and housing consumers, are seriously flawed. The most damaging element is the variable MH definition, which, in essence, is based on the perception of the interviewer or, in cases of self-reporting, the respondent. (This compares with other more precise definitions, which have clear structural attributes.) Furthermore, neither the Census nor the AHS distinguishes "mobile homes" from "trailers." Also, without clear-cut directions for determining structural heritage, units that are inherently MHs may be classified as single-family detached housing units, a misclassification that is especially likely for multisection MHs on individual lots. Given the rapid increase in number and proportion of multisection units over the last several years, this definitional difficulty yields a sizable, systematic bias to both Census and AHS data. Since changes were not made in the 1980 Census to remedy this problem, the limitations inherent in this data source will remain a major constraint on its usefulness.[1]

Table 4–1 summarizes pertinent data from the 1976 AHS. Since condo/cooperative conversion and new construction are relatively recent phenomena, it is reasonable to conclude for these data that siting in groups of six or more covers MH parks. Of that number about two thirds of the units are in parks of 100 or more units. The vast majority of MH units (82 percent) are resident-owned, though an almost equal proportion of the units (76 percent) are located on rented sites. The 1976 AHS reported a median income of $10,000, for owner-occupied MH households, which compared with $14,400 for all owner-occupied households. For renter-occupied households the comparison of median income is $6,900 for MHs and $8,100 for all renter-occupied households.

The extent of the bias in the Census or AHS is difficult to determine since other, private sources of data also have a variety of problems. However, a review of two private data sources gives some indication of the bias in terms of such basic indicators as age, income, family size, and location. One source is a detailed consumer profile compiled for Fleetwood Industries based on survey responses of Fleetwood MH purchasers in the second through fourth quarters of 1978. (Fleetwood is the second largest

Table 4–1   MH Household Data, 1976

Total Occupied MHs	3,627,000
Location	
Urban	31%
Rural	69%
Siting	
Group of six or more	49%
Individual	51%
Home Ownership	
Home owned	82%
Home rented	18%
Home Acquired (Owned Homes)	
New	51%
Resale	49%
Land Ownership	
Site owned	24%
Site rented	76%

Income of Household Heads	Owner Occupied	Renter Occupied
Less than $5,000	21.8%	32.8%
$5,000–6,999	11.1%	18.4%
$7,000–9,999	16.9%	18.9%
$10,000–14,999	27.0%	16.7%
$15,000–24,999	17.7%	10.9%
$25,000 +	5.5%	2.3%
Median	$10,000	$6,900

SOURCE: U.S. Department of Commerce, Bureau of the Census. 1976. *Annual Housing Survey.*

MH producer of units, selling both single- and multisection units throughout the United States.) A second source is a market study of consumer shelter decision making prepared for Owens-Corning, based on data collected in early 1978.[2]

Although the Owens-Corning study did not report a specific median income, the distribution of reported income of MH occupants suggests a figure about $15,000, above that of renters and somewhat below that of all home owners (see Table 4–2). (Home owner median income would fall in the $15,000–19,999 range.) One quarter of MH residents reported income of $20,000 or more, compared with about one third of home owners. Based on this

Table 4–2   Family Income, 1977 (by %)

Income	Home Owners	Renters	MH Residents (Own or Rent)
Under $7,000	4	18	11
$7,000–14,999	33	46	37
$15,000–19,999	32	18	27
$20,000–29,999	23	16	20
$30,000 or more	8	2	5

SOURCE: Owens-Corning. 1978. *Barriers to Greater Sales Growth.* Toledo: Owens-Corning Fiberglas Corp.

source, which lumps MH renters and owners, income of MH residents is neither as low nor as disparate from all home owners as AHS data would indicate.

The Fleetwood data provide some evidence on income, age, and locational characteristics of new MH owners. As compared with other data, Fleetwood's are certain to incorporate owners of both single- and multisection MHs, although the voluntary nature

Table 4–3   Total Annual Family Income, by Household Size and Age of Head of Household, MH Owners

	Household Size			Age of Head of Household		
	All Respondents	Two or Fewer	Three or More	Under 35 Years	35–54 Years Old	55 Years or Over
Sample size	1,869	1,053	772	699	529	609
Under $8,000	11.3%	17.0%	4.0%	4.3%	4.7%	26.2%
$ 8,000–$ 9,999	8.5	10.8	5.6	7.6	5.8	12.2
$10,000–$11,999	11.2	12.8	9.0	13.9	7.2	11.4
$12,000–$13,999	11.7	10.8	12.8	15.8	9.9	8.0
$14,000–$15,999	12.6	9.8	16.0	15.0	14.0	3.2
$16,000–$17,999	9.3	7.8	11.4	10.8	10.5	6.2
$18,000–$19,999	9.1	7.0	12.0	12.1	9.5	5.0
$20,000–$24,999	13.2	12.0	15.0	13.2	17.7	8.8
$25,000 +	13.2	11.8	14.4	7.3	20.6	14.0
No answers	230	148	70	53	44	109
Median	$15,170	$13,724	$16,475	$15,113	$17,588	$12,050

SOURCE: Fleetwood Enterprises. 1978. *Manufactured Home Buyer Profile.* Tustin, Cal.: Product Management Co.

Note: Percentages are based only on those responding.

Table 4-4 Age of Head of Household, MH Owners (in %)

| | Fleetwood | | |
Age	All Households	Households of 3 or More	AHS*
Under 25	14.4	13.6	15.9
25–34	23.6	39.3	28.4
35–44	13.1	22.1	13.3
45–61	28.7	21.8	22.3
62 and over	20.1	3.1	20.1

Sources: U.S. Department of Commerce, Bureau of the Census. 1976. *Annual Housing Survey.*

Fleetwood Enterprises. 1978. *Manufactured Home Buyer Profile.* Tustin, Cal.: Product Management Co.

Note: Percentages may not equal 100 due to rounding. AHS data interpolated to match Fleetwood age categories at upper end.

* Owner-occupied, two-or-more-person households, male head, wife present, no non-relatives.

of response yields its own set of limitations. Table 4–3 presents family income by household size and age of head of household. The reported median income was $15,170, with 57.4 percent reporting income of $14,000 or more and over one quarter of households reporting income of $20,000 or more. The median income in households of three or more persons (that is, families with children) was $16,475, while the median income in households with the head aged 35–54 was $17,588. About 42 percent of the households had three or more persons. Taken together the Fleetwood data suggest that the profile of the MH consumer is beginning to include higher-income families with the head of household in the middle-age range. This aspect constitutes a new consumer group for the MH industry, which traditionally had focused on (and in large part still retains) a large young and retirement family market.

This trend is illustrated in Table 4–4, which compares (after some interpolation to match age groupings) AHS and Fleetwood age of head of household data. Of households of three or more persons in the Fleetwood data, nearly two thirds had a head of household between the ages of 25 and 44. As noted above about two fifths of Fleetwood's buyers were in this category. As shown on Table 4–5, this group also tends to locate its MHs in more traditional private property or subdivision settings.[3]

Table 4–5   Placement of MHs

	Sample Size	MH Park	Private Property	MH Subdivision	No Answers
All Respondents	1,869	50.2%	43.9%	5.9%	36
By Household Size					
One or two	1,053	58.9	35.1	6.0	22
Three or more	772	38.8	55.8	5.4	10
By Age of Household Head					
Under 35 years	699	48.1%	48.3%	3.6%	9
35–54 years	529	43.1	50.2	6.7	7
55 + years	609	59.2	32.7	8.1	16
By Total Annual Income					
Less than $12,000	508	62.6%	33.0%	4.4%	8
$12,000–$19,999	698	46.1	49.1	4.8	6
$20,000 +	433	44.1	45.5	10.4	9

Source: Fleetwood Enterprises. 1978. *Manufactured Home Buyer Profile.* Tustin, Cal.: Product Management Co.

Note: Percentages are based only on those responding.

MH Cost and Value

In 1980 the average sales price of a new MH was $18,500, with the average size 1,050 square feet, for a cost per square foot of $17.80.[3] (Changes in cost and size since 1973 are found in Table 3–5.) However, because of the various settings in which MHs are found, and the consequent differences in associated cost and value, it is necessary to look at several aspects of MH cost and value.

MH Cost

The price quoted for an MH sale is the dealer retail price, covering only the MH unit itself, not transportation costs, site preparation, and unit setup on site.[4] The price is also exclusive of any applicable state or local taxes (Chapter 5 discusses tax status). In 1980 the price range for single-section MHs was $7,500–$25,000, with the average price $15,500. The 1980 range of multisection prices was $17,500–$40,000, with some luxury units costing even larger sums, with the average price $25,000.

The costs of transportation vary depending on distance, with the 1980 average about $1,000. The average distance moved is 300 miles. For example, moving costs for a single-section MH (70 feet by 14 feet) from Erie, Pennsylvania, to Boston, Massachusetts (approximately 500 miles), are approximately $1,275, inclusive of the move, federal fuel tax at 18.5 percent, oversize permits, and escort cars where required.

In addition to transportation, the basic costs prior to occupancy of an MH unit are site preparation and unit setup. The costs vary according to the preferences of the owner, site characteristics, and applicable public regulations; the actual cash outlay may also vary with the amount of work done by the unit owner. Included in site preparation are the following costs: grading; foundation if permanently affixed or "pad" and wind stabilization system provisions if not permanently affixed; utilities; water and sewer (well and septic system unless connected to municipal system); patio and/or porch; outbuildings (shed, garage); paving (streets, walks, driveways); landscaping; and so on. The 1977 estimates of site-preparation costs in an average-sized MH park ranged from $4,500 to $7,000.[5]

Setup involves siting the unit, with all applicable finish and connecting work. Setup costs, charged at $15/person/hour plus materials, depend on conditions. A two-person, eight-hour setup would cost approximately $300.[6] Unit set-up estimates, based on 1981 FHA allowable costs, are $500 for single-section and $1,000 for multisection MHs.

The single largest determinant of MH price is whether the MH is purchased with or without the land on which it is to be sited. This distinction is important in determining the basis for financing, and the subsequent financial responsibilities and advantages of the MH occupant.

MH Subdivisions. The emerging trend toward MH subdivisions represents one end of the price continuum. Here the cost basis for purchase duplicates that of the sale of any form of new single-family detached dwelling. It includes unit cost, transportation, site preparation, setup, taxes, and so on. Illustrative of costs in these situations are subdivisions in Michigan, Washington, Illinois, and California.

Tierra del Sol is a 255-unit subdivision in Bakersfield, California. Its two- and three-bedroom houses, with two-car garages, sell for an average of $50,000; the units range from 960 to 1,800 square feet. Recreational facilities provided include a clubhouse, swimming pool, and whirlpool spa. Maintenance of all exterior facilities is provided through a home owners' association. The developer has arranged a 30-year financing package for purchasers, with provisions for down payments as low as 5 percent of purchase price, with mortgage interest rates from 11 3/4 to 12 3/4 percent (*Manufactured Housing DEALER*, 1980).

Candlewood Glen, in Pierce County near Tacoma, Washington, was the first MH subdivision to obtain FNMA approval for purchase of its paper on the secondary market. Two- and three-bedroom homes, ranging from 900 to 1,850 square feet in this 15-acre, 42-unit subdivision, sell from $50,000 to $69,000 (Carr, 1980).

An MH dealer in Illinois, who has developed five subdivisions, is selling both MH and modular houses in his Rolling Hills development near Urbana. Both about equal size, the MH sells for about $49,000, and the modular $60,000 (Wright, 1981, p. 29). Finally, a major MH manufacturer in Michigan has created a development subsidiary aimed at both the subdivision and the individual lot market. Champion Home Communities has plans for a 193-unit subdivision in Huron County. A basic MH unit retail price of $28,500 to $32,500 is quoted, with the ultimate cost to the buyer (inclusive of land and site preparation) ranging from the upper $30,000s to the upper $40,000s, depending on the land cost to the buyer (Wright, 1981). As indicated by both the Illinois and Michigan developments, the cost differential between MHs and other forms of single-family housing in subdivisions is due to the lower initial cost of the MH unit, even including its transportation and setup costs. Once permanently sited, these units will qualify for conventional shelter loans.

MH Parks. The opposite end of the continuum from the MH subdivision is the MH park. As compared with the MH subdivision, characterized by larger and multisection MHs, the MH park is more likely to have single-section MHs—which alone lowers the housing cost to the occupant. Also, because the MH occupant rents the land, the land and improvements costs are not included in the amount financed although these costs are passed along in the rent for space. Table 4–6 presents a cost comparison for home

Table 4–6 New Hampshire Home Ownership Cost Comparison, March 1980

	MH in Park		Site-Built SFD	
	New	*Existing*	*New*	*Existing*
Purchase Price	$20,000	$12,000	$65,000	$45,000
Financing				
Term of mortgage/loan	10 yrs.	7 yrs.	30 yrs.	30 yrs.
Interest rate	15%	16.5%	15%	15%
Down payment	$ 5,000	$ 3,000	$13,000	$ 9,000
Amount financed	$15,000	$ 9,000	$52,000	$36,000
Monthly Housing Costs				
Principal and interest	$ 242	$ 181	$ 657	$ 455
Park rent	100	80	—	—
Property taxes	38	23	126	86
Insurance	16	11	25	16
Heat and utilities	90	90	110	110
Water	— in rent —		10	10
Maintenance	10	10	27	37
Comprehensive Monthly Housing Cost	$ 496	$ 395	$ 955	$ 714
Estimated Annual Income Needed to Support	$17,856	$14,220	$34,380	$25,704

SOURCE: Adapted from *New Hampshire Mobile Home Study.* 1980. Concord, N.H.: Office of State Planning.

Notes: 1. Estimated monthly rent for new park is $100; average for existing parks is about $80.
2. Annual taxes computed at fair market value, taxed at 1978 New Hampshire average equalized rate of 0.023 percent (2.3 percent of market value).
3. Heat and utilities costs based on NHHC Section 8 monthly utility allowance averages. Average rates for two- to three-bedroom apartments were applied to MHs; averages for four-bedroom apartment used for conventional single family.
4. Annual maintenance cost estimated at ½ of 1 percent of fair market value for new homes; 1 percent of market value used for existing homes.
5. Estimated annual income necessary based on household spending one third of income on monthly housing costs.

ownership of MHs and site-built single-family dwellings in New Hampshire, prepared as part of an MH study by the New Hampshire Housing Commission. It illustrates for that state monthly housing costs associated with the purchase of typical new and existing MHs and site-built SFDs. One can assume a relative equivalency of housing cost for MHs not affixed on owned land with those for MHs in parks. Park rent equates with land and improvements costs of such units on owned land. Affixed MHs will have a higher property tax, since the fair market value of the two combined will exceed that of the two taken separately. The least-cost assumption would involve a low-priced, single-section MH not affixed on the owner's land. Inclusive of unit cost, land cost, all site preparation, transportation and setup, it is possible for the final price to be less than $20,000, perhaps as low as $15,000.[7]

Financing. Table 4–6 also illustrates one of the basic differences between MHs treated as real or personal property—namely, the terms of the financing. Because MH units traditionally have not been affixed to the land on which they are located, and because in half the cases the land is not owned by the unit owner, financing has necessarily been on a personal property, installment loan basis. The loan is secured either as personal credit or, more commonly, with the MH unit offered as the security for a chattel mortgage. Financing as an installment loan has meant shorter terms for maturity and, until the recent escalation in mortgage interest rates, significantly higher interest rates. (Installment loans still have a higher rate although the differential is not as great.) Further, the installment loans have been placed with "add-on" interest, in which the amount of interest is calculated on the total note and added on to the initial proceeds to determine total payback. This method compares with mortgage calculation, which is on a "simple interest" basis, with interest calculated on the balance outstanding since the preceding payment. The result is a higher monthly payment on principal and interest for traditional MH loans than for an equivalent dollar amount on conventional shelter loan terms. Although there is a distinct trend toward a simple interest basis, less than half of financing institutions in MHI's 1980 survey made use of the simple interest method.[8]

Tables 4–7 and 4–8 present data on minimum down payment and average maturities of new loans during the period 1976–1980.

Table 4–7 Minimum Acceptable Down Payment Required by Financial Institutions for MHs, 1976–1980 (in %)

MH	1976	1977	1978	1979	1980
Single-section, new	15.88	16.28	16.96	18.36	17.78
Single-section, existing	18.91	18.73	19.31	21.13	20.08
Multisection, new	16.73	17.50	17.97	19.25	18.74
Multisection, existing	19.14	19.26	20.27	21.61	20.95

SOURCE: Manufactured Housing Institute. 1976, 1981. *Manufactured Home Financing.*

Table 4–8 Average Maturity on New MH Loans, 1976–1980 (in months)

MH	1976	1977	1978	1979	1980
Single-section, new	113.45	115.9	120.71	124.44	132.49
Single-section, existing	74.94	75.0	80.85	80.9	89.0
Multisection, new	136.0	138.4	144.87	142.04	154.0
Multisection, existing	93.64	97.4	105.4	102.03	112.21

SOURCE: Manufactured Housing Institute. 1976, 1981. *Manufactured Home Financing.*

Both have increased over this time period. It is important to note that these data do not distinguish between mortgage financing and installment loan basis. The 1980 MHI survey noted that over one half of reporting institutions provided maximum maturities of more than 144 months on new multisection MHs, with 90.2 percent of S&Ls in this category (MHI, 1980, p. 19). These longer maturities, combined with use of simple interest method, are reflective of the increasing proportion of MH loans made on a real property basis.

MH purchasers can also make use of VA and FHA programs. The FHA program insures the loan, whereas the VA either insures the loan or provides a direct loan. (Terms of the programs as of June 1981 are shown in Table 6–4, in Chapter 6.) Lenders have made increasing use of the FHA and VA programs to protect their MH loan portfolios. In MHI's 1976 survey, 8.1 percent used FHA insurance, and 6.5 percent used the VA guaranty (MHI, 1976, p. 30). By the 1980 survey, 19.3 percent of lenders used FHA insurance, and 14.8 percent the VA guaranty (MHI, 1980, p. 19).[9]

Use of either the VA or FHA programs provides for longer maturities, lower down payments, and, often, lower interest rates and amounts. In the New Hampshire study, from which Table 4–6 was drawn, it was calculated that it was possible to reduce to as low as $12,100 the annual income requirements to purchase an existing MH, depending on the mix of program, down payment, rate, and maturity (New Hampshire Housing Commission, 1980, pp. 15–16). The obvious benefit of the lower down payment requirements is that a purchaser need not have accumulated as large an initial equity before purchasing an MH. It is the combination of the lower initial price and lower equity requirement that has enabled younger families with lower incomes to achieve home ownership of MHs through FHA or VA programs.

MH Value

An issue related to purchase financing is the determination of value, notably for existing MHs. Historically, MHs have been assumed to depreciate. Value was calculated in a manner similar to that for used cars, with a book relating manufacturer, model, and year of construction to a present value. A parallel method applied a fixed rate of depreciation (typically 10 percent annually) down to a minimum residual value. (As will be noted in Chapter 5, many states continue to use one or a combination of these methods to determine a taxable value.)

This traditional approach to determining value is being abandoned due to a variety of factors. Foremost among these factors

Table 4–9 Multisection MH Appreciation, 24′ Wide (in %)

Year Constructed	Year Sold							
	1972	1973	1974	1975	1976	1977	1978	2nd Qtr. 1979
1971	96	91	98	115	117	138	129	133
1972		98	91	111	113	120	132	142
1973			101	102	108	116	128	130
1974				106	103	108	123	121
1975					105	105	113	120
1976						104	115	115
1977							111	112
1978								104

SOURCE: Malnight, Jim. 1980. "Mobile Homes Appreciate in Value," *Manufactured Housing DEALER*. January, p. 20.

is mounting evidence that MHs appreciate rather than depreciate in value. Contributing to the appreciation phenomenon are increased average size, increased proportion of multisection MHs, decreased frequency of movement, and improved, assured construction quality.

An ongoing study by the Foremost Insurance Company involving approximately 620,000 MH units has found that both single- and multisection MHs appreciate, though not at the same rate. Tables 4–9, 4–10, and 4–11 present Foremost's findings through the second quarter of 1979 for two widths of single-

Table 4–10   Single-Section MH Appreciation, 12′ Wide (in %)

Year Constructed	Year Sold							
	1972	1973	1974	1975	1976	1977	1978	2nd Qtr. 1979
1971	96	88	83	98	100	96	99	106
1972		99	91	96	97	99	103	107
1973			101	104	106	101	104	110
1974				107	105	100	101	102
1975					96	93	96	97
1976						103	95	96
1977							100	98
1978								103

SOURCE: Malnight, Jim. 1980. "Mobile Homes Appreciate in Value," *Manufactured Housing DEALER*. January, p. 17.

Table 4–11   Single-Section MH Appreciation, 14′ Wide (in %)

Year Constructed	Year Sold							
	1972	1973	1974	1975	1976	1977	1978	2nd Qtr. 1979
1971	96	83	96	84	88	91	98	106
1972		96	90	91	95	99	98	98
1973			96	97	101	88	97	101
1974				102	96	95	96	102
1975					103	99	97	102
1976						104	98	97
1977							103	101
1978								104

SOURCE: Malnight, Jim. 1980. "Mobile Homes Appreciate in Value," *Manufactured Housing DEALER*. January, p. 18.

section MHs and for multisection MHs. It should be noted that these data tend to reflect MHs that remain in a personal property category and, hence, are more likely to be found in MH parks.[10] The conclusions, therefore, probably underestimate the appreciation of permanently sited MHs, which tend to exhibit value characteristics common to similarly sized and sited single-family detached dwellings.

Foremost was able to categorize states into three groups (for both single- and multisection homes) according to appreciation (Figure 4–1). The first group, rapid appreciation, included seven states, all but two on the West Coast. In these states MHs appreciated from 4 percent to 7 percent annually, and one, California, showed a 10 percent to 15 percent annual rate. The other six states were Alaska, Arizona, Florida, New Jersey, Oregon, and Washington. The second group, steady increase, included twenty-

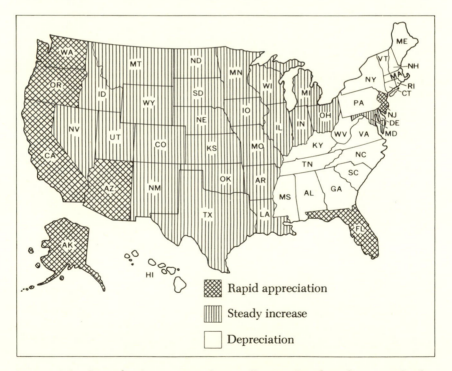

Figure 4–1   States by Appreciation Status. *(Source: Based on data in Malnight, Jim. 1980. "Mobile Homes Appreciate in Value,"* Manufactured Housing DEALER, *January, pp. 16–18.)*

five states, all but two in the central part of the country. MHs in these states exhibited values either slightly below or above new home costs. Three states, Michigan, Wisconsin and Minnesota, seemed likely to move into the rapid appreciation group. The other 22 states were Ohio, Illinois, Indiana, North Dakota, South Dakota, Iowa, Nebraska, Kansas, Missouri, Arkansas, Oklahoma, Texas, Colorado, Wyoming, Idaho, Utah, New Mexico, Nevada, Montana, Louisiana, Connecticut, and Maryland. The third group, depreciation, included 17 states, all found in the eastern part of the United States. These states showed a level of 85 percent of original value, although a study three years previously had indicated values in the 60 percent range, suggesting upward movement in value even in these states. The 17 states are Maine, Vermont, Delaware, Rhode Island, New York, Pennsylvania, North Carolina, Virginia, New Hampshire, South Carolina, Tennessee, Alabama, Georgia, Mississippi, Kentucky, West Virginia, and Massachusetts. (Hawaii was not included in the analysis.)

Perhaps the most important conclusion of the Foremost study is the summary of factors influencing the value of MHs. Five factors were noted: (1) location, (2) upkeep and maintenance, (3) original quality of the home, (4) supply and demand for housing within a particular area, and (5) turnover rate for homes within an area (Malnight, p. 24). None of these factors is surprising to persons familiar with real estate. Indeed, the finding is indicative of the increasingly recognized reality that MHs are part of the housing market, rather than definitionally depreciable consumer products.

This finding has led to new appraisal practices based on more traditional real estate standards (*Banking*, 1978; Roode, 1980; Beverly, 1980). Whereas recently constructed, permanently sited MHs can be appraised using standard residential appraisal practices, older MHs and those on rented land do present unique circumstances. The variations in construction quality prior to the HUD Code, both by manufacturer and year of construction, present particular challenges to the appraiser in determining remaining useful life. Similarly, the variations in legal right to tenancy of rented space creates appraisal complications. Neither of these areas has been sufficiently sorted out to yield standard appraisal practices. However, the increasing frequency of trade journal articles on this topic, usually accompanied by the forms used by the author's company, is indicative of the rapid shift to real estate appraisal practices in determining value of MHs.

MH Market Activity

Although there are major problems in adequacy of aggregate MH national data concerning their location and characteristics of occupants, the problems are less severe in terms of numbers of units. Because the overwhelming number of MH units produced before 1970 were single-section units, the 1970 Census data provide a reasonable (though not wholly adequate) base for establishing occupied MH units in that year. Because the MH industry has relatively few firms, it has been able to track unit production annually, including the states to which units are shipped. (Here shipments are the equivalent of "starts" for site-built housing.) Moreover, since the imposition of federal construction standards, shipment data are maintained as part of the HUD program.

Table 4–12 presents a state-by-state estimate of MH housing stock for the years 1970 to 1980. In 1970 it is estimated that 2.35 million units were in the year-round MH housing stock; that number had risen to approximately 3.83 million by the end of 1980. The one caution about the estimates for the later years is that they were made on the assumption that only 93.5 percent of each year's shipments enter the primary, year-round MH housing stock and that there is an annual 5 percent outflow rate (T&E, 1980*c*, p. 145). These assumptions were applied uniformly to each state for each year. Although this model of MH market activity seems to be substantiated for the first half of the decade, it probably underestimates full-time additions to and overestimates outflows from the MH housing stock for the latter half of the decade. The underestimation results from not accounting for changes in MHs in the late 1970s—notably the larger proportion of multi-section units, which are almost exclusively entering the stock of full-time occupied units, and the presumed better durability of units produced, and hence lower removals from stock due to physical deterioration. Thus the stock estimates for the more recent years need to be used judiciously, certainly for the aggregate, and absolutely for the individual states.

Table 4–12 Estimated Stock of Year-Round Occupied MHs at Year's End, 1970–1980

State	1970	1971	1972	1973	1974	1975	1976	1977	1978	1979	1980
AL	60,274	72,219	87,008	104,194	109,391	109,265	109,760	104,272	106,758	109,286	108,764
AK	10,944	11,303	11,326	11,704	12,369	14,270	14,210	14,215	13,971	13,403	12,834
AZ	57,624	70,993	87,501	102,813	106,379	105,147	104,064	104,711	106,704	109,740	109,300
AR	32,450	38,887	45,758	52,974	56,197	57,025	57,729	57,616	57,189	56,758	56,170
CA	204,325	224,569	245,352	258,009	263,883	266,978	273,559	286,888	292,367	293,434	290,081
CO	35,982	44,158	52,215	56,956	57,500	56,894	57,100	54,245	55,687	57,087	56,800
CT	10,049	10,225	10,257	10,405	10,473	10,318	10,184	10,017	9,842	9,660	9,459
DE	10,563	11,842	13,643	15,496	16,445	16,798	17,367	17,661	17,925	18,213	18,284
FL	198,289	234,532	273,282	312,604	322,147	319,612	317,767	317,708	321,782	332,297	340,337
GA	94,602	111,210	129,885	149,240	153,898	152,718	154,021	153,349	153,770	155,373	155,526
HI	175	207	258	245	248	236	243	231	219	208	198
ID	18,565	21,521	25,110	27,645	29,585	30,996	33,220	34,599	35,734	36,586	36,228
IL	79,677	86,621	94,864	102,775	104,975	105,502	106,212	106,125	105,233	104,010	101,655
IN	77,070	87,124	96,751	104,834	106,597	105,526	104,933	104,601	104,970	105,120	103,861
IA	27,355	30,465	32,570	34,545	35,541	36,208	37,332	38,280	38,320	38,172	37,813
KS	30,317	33,644	37,819	41,507	43,448	45,295	47,568	48,396	48,546	48,843	48,504
KY	48,474	57,328	66,876	75,917	78,704	79,993	81,355	83,360	84,468	85,855	85,289
LA	42,555	48,221	57,946	68,396	73,121	74,982	77,914	83,682	90,492	96,576	103,084
ME	20,220	22,617	24,524	26,590	27,300	26,904	26,704	26,675	26,668	26,504	25,937
MA	11,801	12,378	12,845	13,499	13,720	13,621	13,650	13,558	13,500	13,338	13,136
MD	22,035	23,201	24,648	26,233	27,055	26,996	26,996	26,724	26,491	26,181	25,892
MI	89,740	106,653	121,641	135,188	137,717	135,288	133,456	134,353	136,091	136,506	133,720
MN	35,052	39,642	43,663	48,339	51,316	53,594	56,607	58,103	58,720	58,583	57,038
MS	35,347	42,541	53,651	67,192	71,811	70,608	70,144	69,961	70,405	71,226	71,219
MO	56,622	63,293	73,204	81,302	83,359	83,814	84,958	84,993	84,913	84,732	83,602
MT	18,568	20,878	23,792	25,894	27,345	27,782	28,752	30,363	31,473	31,933	31,636
NE	16,966	19,584	21,899	23,748	24,542	24,829	25,457	25,957	26,046	26,018	25,577

Table 4–12 (cont.)

State	1970	1971	1972	1973	1974	1975	1976	1977	1978	1979	1980
NV	21,468	22,803	24,846	27,111	27,683	27,525	27,434	28,937	30,427	31,582	31,564
NH	14,120	15,266	16,304	17,531	17,973	17,902	17,812	17,853	17,873	17,748	17,509
NJ	16,876	18,070	18,852	19,645	20,110	20,316	24,073	20,387	20,259	20,013	19,647
NM	20,533	24,327	30,281	37,387	41,056	41,741	42,360	44,930	47,166	48,299	48,281
NY	86,480	93,444	100,127	107,093	109,115	107,088	105,735	104,216	102,483	100,947	98,767
NC	115,425	135,315	162,092	183,800	192,861	192,083	193,088	192,893	193,582	195,888	196,197
ND	10,515	12,146	13,350	14,585	15,377	16,485	17,998	18,561	18,956	19,232	19,334
OH	98,164	110,408	122,286	132,718	135,947	135,387	135,256	135,374	135,102	135,696	134,366
OK	30,767	36,037	42,875	47,905	50,066	50,465	51,865	53,121	55,967	58,917	61,844
OR	40,992	50,567	60,483	71,411	75,979	78,163	82,167	85,431	88,226	84,406	84,047
PA	100,763	112,960	128,588	143,011	148,077	148,280	149,612	150,838	150,235	149,431	146,768
RI	2,528	2,678	2,811	2,952	3,054	2,995	2,909	2,842	2,778	2,717	2,638
SC	57,946	66,515	79,914	95,206	101,706	101,450	102,702	103,071	103,840	105,546	105,604
SD	12,934	14,468	17,082	18,543	19,152	19,179	19,418	19,641	19,660	19,478	19,097
TN	54,433	65,937	79,021	92,625	95,577	94,051	92,903	92,750	92,772	93,046	92,374
TX	115,072	140,743	175,134	198,690	208,291	213,485	223,550	232,550	244,464	256,621	268,328
UT	10,286	12,086	15,267	17,960	19,110	19,505	19,984	20,520	21,134	21,491	21,450
VT	10,513	11,151	11,437	11,779	11,588	11,361	11,195	11,049	10,972	10,905	10,743
VA	57,062	64,047	72,876	79,914	83,317	82,948	83,009	83,576	83,894	84,281	83,760
WA	46,694	51,437	56,673	64,433	70,724	75,855	81,945	88,330	94,701	99,938	101,810
WV	31,023	35,692	42,026	47,033	48,876	50,438	52,051	53,758	55,061	56,199	56,225
WI	33,733	38,422	43,359	48,545	50,518	51,461	53,128	53,737	54,008	53,120	52,270
WY	11,152	11,785	12,924	14,004	15,188	15,595	15,974	16,988	17,934	18,796	19,760
Total	2,351,820	2,632,159	3,096,896	3,472,122	3,606,412	3,624,956	3,673,830	3,721,998	3,779,785	3,819,089	3,834,327

Source: Technology and Economics. 1980. *Economic Cost-Benefit and Risk Analysis of Results of Mobile Home Safety Research: Fire Safety.* Washington, D.C.: HUD.

Note: Updated 1978 through 1980 using T&E method and NCSBCS MH series data.

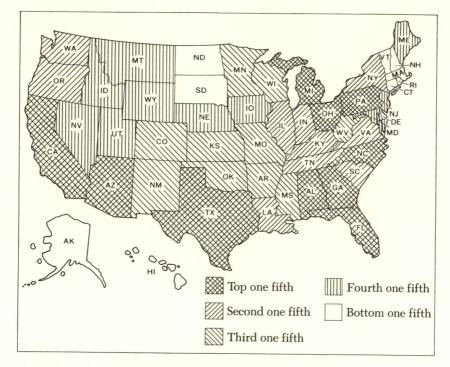

Figure 4–2 States Ranked by Estimate of Year-Round MHs Occupied, 1980 (by Quintile).

Figure 4–2 illustrates the ranking of states by quintiles for full-time occupied MH units in 1980. The states forming the top quintile, with about 1.88 million MH units, have approximately one half of all occupied MH units in the United States (see Table 4–13). Four of these states (Florida, North Carolina,

Table 4–13 States Ranked by Estimate of Year-Round Occupied MHs, 1980

Rank	State	MH Units	Quintile Total	%	Cum. Total	Cum. %
1	Florida	340,337				
2	California	290,081				
3	Texas	268,328				
4	North Carolina	196,196				
5	Georgia	155,526				
6	Pennsylvania	146,768				
7	Ohio	134,366				
8	Michigan	133,720				
9	Arizona	109,300				
10	Alabama	108,764	1,883,386	49.1	1,883,386	49.1

Table 4–13 (cont.)

Rank	State	MH Units	Quintile Total	%	Cum. Total	Cum. %
11	South Carolina	105,604				
12	Indiana	103,861				
13	Louisiana	103,084				
14	Washington	101,810				
15	Illinois	101,655				
16	New York	98,767				
17	Tennessee	92,374				
18	Kentucky	85,289				
19	Oregon	84,047				
20	Virginia	83,760	960,025	25.0	2,842,637	74.1
21	Missouri	83,602				
22	Mississippi	71,219				
23	Oklahoma	61,844				
24	Minnesota	57,038				
25	Colorado	56,800				
26	West Virginia	56,225				
27	Arkansas	56,170				
28	Wisconsin	53,270				
29	Kansas	48,504				
30	New Mexico	48,281	592,953	15.5	3,436,590	89.6
31	Iowa	37,813				
32	Idaho	36,228				
33	Montana	31,636				
34	Nevada	31,564				
35	Maine	25,937				
36	Maryland	25,892				
37	Nebraska	25,577				
38	Utah	21,450				
39	Wyoming	19,760				
40	New Jersey	19,647	275,504	7.2	3,712,094	96.8
41	North Dakota	19,334				
42	South Dakota	19,097				
43	Delaware	18,284				
44	New Hampshire	17,509				
45	Massachusetts	13,136				
46	Alaska	12,834				
47	Vermont	10,743				
48	Connecticut	9,459				
49	Rhode Island	2,638				
50	Hawaii	198	123,232	3.2	3,834,327	100.0

SOURCE: T&E, 1980*c*; NCSBCS.

Georgia, and Alabama) are in the Southeast; one (Texas) is in the South; two (California and Arizona) are in the West; and three (Pennsylvania, Ohio, and Michigan) are in the Midwest. However, only five of these states (not surprisingly the five largest in occupied units) ranked in the first quintile in shipments for each of the four full years since implementation of the HUD Code. Table 4–14 presents shipment data by state for the period 1977–1980. Two states, Washington and Louisiana, were in the first quintile in shipments for the four-year period and in the second quintile in occupied units for 1980. The first two quintiles constitute about three fourths of all occupied MH units in 1980. Eighteen of these states also ranked in the first two quintiles in shipments from 1977 to 1980, indicating a relative stability in distribution of MH use by state. Tables 4–15 through 4–18 present ranking by year.

Only five states had more than 50 percent of their shipments as multisections during the period 1977–1980. Three, California, Florida and Nevada, had more than 50 percent multisection shipments all four years. The other two, Washington and Oregon, had greater than 50 percent multisection shipments for 1978 to 1980. The five states accounted for 56 percent of all multisection shipments in 1980. About two thirds of all shipments to the five states in 1980 were multisection MHs. Figure 4–3 illustrates states with more than 50 percent of shipments as multisections.

Interestingly, the pattern of MH use by state as a proportion of population yields a rather different picture from either shipment or aggregate use data. Table 4–19 presents states ranked by MH units per 100,000 population in 1980. Only 3 of the states ranked in the first quintile for total year-round occupied MHs (Florida, North Carolina, and Arizona) also rank in the top ten states in MH units per 100,000 population. Several of the states in the top quintile in total use, including Texas, California, Pennsylvania, Ohio, and Michigan, rank 30th or lower in use as a proportion of population. Among the top-ranking states in use by population are several which are more rural in character, including top-ranked Wyoming, Montana, Nevada, Idaho, and Alaska. Figure 4–4 displays states by five categories (by thousands of units per 100,000 population) from those with fewer than 1,000 units (N = 8) to those with 4,000+ MH units per 100,000 population (N = 3).

Table 4–14 MH Shipments by State, 1977–1980

State	1977			1978			1979			1980		
	SS	MS	Total	SS	MS	Total	SS	MS	Total	SS	MS	Total
AL	5,881	1,641	7,522	7,005	1,663	8,668	7,207	1,648	8,855	4,641	923	5,564
AK	699	89	788	454	72	526	101	46	147	96	18	114
AZ	3,575	2,721	6,296	4,231	3,907	8,138	5,193	4,231	9,424	3,265	2,417	5,682
AR	2,658	494	3,152	2,345	417	2,762	2,342	392	2,734	2,164	369	2,533
CA	6,277	22,767	29,044	4,651	17,666	22,317	3,596	14,073	17,659	2,127	10,616	12,743
CO	2,866	823	3,689	3,337	1,240	4,677	3,481	1,230	4,711	2,233	657	2,890
CT	357	10	367	354	13	367	333	16	349	304	13	317
DE	1,128	170	1,298	1,122	169	1,291	1,181	152	1,333	972	133	1,105
FL	5,761	11,456	17,217	8,580	13,891	22,471	12,057	18,007	30,064	12,646	15,111	27,757
GA	4,622	3,071	7,693	5,500	3,606	9,106	6,753	3,707	10,460	6,012	2,907	8,919
HI	0	0	0	0	0	0	0	0	0	0	0	0
ID	2,241	1,058	3,299	2,165	1,160	3,325	1,787	1,184	1,971	966	690	1,656
IL	4,659	1,120	5,779	4,097	873	4,970	3,878	669	4,547	2,710	494	3,204
IN	4,589	845	5,434	5,618	686	6,304	5,450	628	6,078	4,042	458	4,500
IA	2,738	323	3,061	1,938	262	2,300	1,778	212	1,990	1,449	295	1,744
KS	2,903	595	3,498	2,357	536	2,893	2,597	470	3,067	1,988	380	2,368
KY	5,631	1,232	6,863	4,920	1,020	5,940	5,418	898	6,316	3,699	497	4,196
LA	9,963	667	10,630	11,349	1,028	12,377	11,061	882	11,943	12,024	739	12,763
ME	1,380	46	1,426	1,468	26	1,494	1,286	31	1,317	844	10	854
MD	1,107	102	1,209	1,109	133	1,242	1,032	110	1,142	1,007	141	1,148
MA	586	50	636	644	54	698	569	65	634	458	65	523
MI	7,289	977	8,266	8,439	1,080	9,519	7,133	995	8,128	4,037	510	4,547
MN	4,184	537	4,721	3,363	602	3,965	2,660	491	3,151	1,342	216	1,558
MS	3,113	613	3,726	3,729	709	4,438	4,297	590	4,887	3,469	533	4,002
MO	3,606	1,185	4,791	3,651	1,043	4,694	3,689	887	4,576	2,925	573	3,498

MT	2,812	497	3,309	2,426	533	2,959	1,871	418	2,289	1,177	286	1,463
NE	1,565	366	1,931	1,197	364	1,561	1,086	349	1,435	770	198	968
NV	1,457	1,652	3,109	1,296	2,010	3,306	1,120	1,893	3,013	726	1,032	1,758
NH	973	51	1,024	960	67	1,027	805	60	865	691	39	730
NJ	801	205	1,006	774	230	1,004	681	183	864	555	160	715
NM	4,402	712	5,114	4,156	890	5,046	3,042	888	3,930	2,116	583	2,699
NY	3,744	424	4,168	3,441	474	3,915	3,665	375	4,040	2,963	365	3,228
NC	8,076	2,505	10,578	8,818	2,816	11,634	10,469	3,021	13,493	9,363	2,012	11,375
ND	1,369	231	1,600	1,202	288	1,490	1,075	303	1,378	1,022	175	1,197
OH	6,181	1,278	7,459	6,100	1,214	7,314	7,129	1,145	8,274	5,351	790	6,141
OK	3,829	408	4,237	5,554	640	6,194	5,741	730	6,471	5,914	698	6,612
OR	4,192	3,805	7,997	3,165	4,792	7,956	2,676	4,290	6,966	1,498	2,849	4,347
PA	8,558	1,154	9,712	6,809	1,003	7,812	6,753	799	7,552	4,927	487	5,414
RI	88	1	89	85	3	88	82	6	88	50	14	64
SC	4,275	1,835	6,110	4,564	2,104	6,668	5,519	2,247	7,766	4,522	1,485	6,007
SD	1,132	184	1,316	969	158	1,127	724	178	902	546	121	667
TN	3,930	1,090	5,020	4,204	1,042	5,246	4,470	1,061	5,531	3,811	670	4,481
TX	19,439	2,609	22,048	23,099	3,404	26,503	23,484	3,964	27,448	23,698	3,927	27,625
UT	1,101	555	1,656	1,208	638	1,846	1,027	564	1,591	720	444	1,164
VT	441	28	459	525	10	535	528	14	542	419	13	432
VA	4,234	1,235	5,469	3,992	1,070	5,062	4,261	897	5,158	3,540	618	4,158
WA	6,153	5,209	11,362	5,380	6,755	12,145	4,772	6,455	11,227	3,232	4,501	7,733
WV	4,136	684	4,820	3,753	740	4,493	3,805	576	4,381	2,847	346	3,193
WI	2,775	281	3,056	3,052	278	3,330	2,768	173	2,941	1,952	81	2,033
WY	1,681	286	1,967	1,648	373	2,021	1,605	375	1,980	1,705	438	2,143
D.C. and U.S. Terr.	4	1	5	2	0	2	0	0	0	0	36	36
Total	185,651	79,859	265,510	190,838	83,862	274,700	194,075	82,805	276,880	160,352	61,255	221,607

SOURCE: NCSBCS, MH Series.

Table 4–15   Rank, Number, and Percentage of Total Shipments, by State, 1977

Rank	State	Shipments	Percent of Total
1	California	29,044	10.9
2	Texas	22,048	8.2
3	Florida	17,217	5.1
4	Washington	11,362	4.3
5	Louisiana	10,630	4.0
6	North Carolina	10,578	4.0
7	Pennsylvania	9,712	3.7
8	Michigan	8,266	3.1
9	Oregon	7,997	3.0
10	Georgia	7,693	2.9
11	Alabama	7,522	2.8
12	Ohio	7,459	2.8
13	Kentucky	6,863	2.6
14	Arizona	6,296	2.4
15	South Carolina	6,110	2.3
16	Illinois	5,779	2.2
17	Virginia	5,469	2.1
18	Indiana	5,434	2.0
19	New Mexico	5,114	1.9
20	Tennessee	5,020	1.9
21	West Virginia	4,820	1.8
22	Missouri	4,791	1.8
23	Minnesota	4,721	1.8
24	Oklahoma	4,237	1.6
25	New York	4,168	1.6
26	Mississippi	3,726	1.4
27	Colorado	3,689	1.4
28	Kansas	3,498	1.3
29	Montana	3,309	1.2
30	Idaho	3,299	1.2
31	Arkansas	3,152	1.2
32	Nevada	3,109	1.2
33	Iowa	3,061	1.2
34	Wisconsin	3,056	1.2
35	Wyoming	1,967	0.7
36	Nebraska	1,931	0.7
37	Utah	1,656	0.6
38	North Dakota	1,600	0.6
39	Maine	1,426	0.5
40	South Dakota	1,316	0.5
41	Delaware	1,298	0.5
42	Maryland	1,209	0.5

Table 4–15 (cont.)

Rank	State	Shipments	Percent of Total
43	New Hampshire	1,024	0.4
44	New Jersey	1,006	0.4
45	Alaska	788	0.3
46	Massachusetts	636	0.2
47	Vermont	459	0.2
48	Connecticut	367	0.1
49	Rhode Island	89	0.0
50	D.C. and U.S. Terr.	5	0.0
51	Hawaii	0	0.0

SOURCE: NCSBCS, MH Series.

Note: Percentages do not total 100 due to rounding.

Table 4–16   Rank, Number, and Percentage of Total Shipments, by State, 1978

Rank	State	Shipments	Percent of Total
1	Texas	26,503	9.6
2	Florida	22,471	8.2
3	California	22,317	8.1
4	Louisiana	12,377	4.5
5	Washington	12,145	4.4
6	North Carolina	11,634	4.2
7	Michigan	9,519	3.5
8	Georgia	9,106	3.3
9	Alabama	8,668	3.2
10	Arizona	8,138	3.0
11	Oregon	7,956	2.9
12	Pennsylvania	7,812	2.8
13	Ohio	7,214	2.7
14	South Carolina	6,668	2.4
15	Indiana	6,304	2.3
16	Oklahoma	6,194	2.3
17	Kentucky	5,940	2.2
18	Tennessee	5,246	1.9
19	Virginia	5,062	1.8
20	New Mexico	5,046	1.8
21	Illinois	4,970	1.8
22	Missouri	4,694	1.7
23	Colorado	4,677	1.7
24	West Virginia	4,493	1.6
25	Mississippi	4,438	1.6
26	Minnesota	3,965	1.4

Table 4–16 (cont.)

Rank	State	Shipments	Percent of Total
27	New York	3,915	1.4
28	Wisconsin	3,330	1.2
29	Idaho	3,325	1.2
30	Nevada	3,306	1.2
31	Montana	2,959	1.1
32	Kansas	2,893	1.1
33	Arkansas	2,762	1.0
34	Iowa	2,300	0.8
35	Wyoming	2,021	0.7
36	Utah	1,846	0.7
37	Nebraska	1,561	0.6
38	Maine	1,494	0.5
39	North Dakota	1,490	0.5
40	Delaware	1,291	0.5
41	Maryland	1,242	0.5
42	South Dakota	1,127	0.4
43	New Hampshire	1,027	0.4
44	New Jersey	1,004	0.4
45	Massachusetts	698	0.3
46	Vermont	535	0.2
47	Alaska	526	0.2
48	Connecticut	367	0.1
49	Rhode Island	88	0.0
50	D.C. and U.S. Terr.	2	0.0
51	Hawaii	0	0.0

Source: NCSBCS, MH Series.

Note: Percentages dc not total 100 due to rounding.

Table 4–17   Rank, Number, and Percentage of Total Shipments, by State, 1979

Rank	State	Number	Percent of Total
1	Florida	29,807	10.8
2	Texas	26,886	9.7
3	California	17,572	6.4
4	North Carolina	13,228	4.8
5	Louisiana	11,656	4.2
6	Washington	11,038	4.0
7	Georgia	10,378	3.8
8	Arizona	9,371	3.4
9	Alabama	8,561	3.1
10	Idaho	8,188	3.0

Table 4–17 (cont.)

Rank	State	Number	Percent of Total
11	Michigan	8,036	2.9
12	South Carolina	7,649	2.8
13	Ohio	7,413	2.7
14	Pennsylvania	7,374	2.7
15	Oregon	6,906	2.5
16	Oklahoma	6,259	2.3
17	Kentucky	6,066	2.2
18	Indiana	5,951	2.2
19	Tennessee	5,335	1.9
20	Virginia	5,003	1.8
21	Mississippi	4,796	1.7
22	Colorado	4,624	1.7
23	Illinois	4,474	1.6
24	Missouri	4,451	1.6
25	West Virginia	4,255	1.5
26	New York	3,923	1.4
27	New Mexico	3,868	1.4
28	Wisconsin	3,172	1.1
29	Minnesota	3,112	1.1
30	Nevada	3,012	1.1
31	Kansas	2,987	1.1
32	Arkansas	2,685	1.0
33	Montana	2,266	0.8
34	Iowa	1,955	0.7
35	Wyoming	1,938	0.7
36	Utah	1,567	0.6
37	Nebraska	1,390	0.5
38	North Dakota	1,341	0.5
39	Delaware	1,295	0.5
40	Maine	1,293	0.5
41	Maryland	1,113	0.4
42	South Dakota	889	0.3
43	New Jersey	885	0.3
44	New Hampshire	852	0.3
45	Massachusetts	631	0.2
46	Vermont	527	0.2
47	Connecticut	341	0.1
48	Alaska	145	0.05
49	Rhode Island	86	0.03
50	D.C. and U.S. Terr.	0	0
51	Hawaii	0	0

SOURCE: NCSBCS, MH Series.

Note: Percentages do not total 100 due to rounding.

Table 4–18   Rank, Number, and Percentage of Total Shipments, by State, 1980

Rank	State	Shipments	Percent of Total
1	Florida	27,757	12.5
2	Texas	27,625	12.5
3	Louisiana	12,763	5.8
4	California	12,743	5.8
5	North Carolina	11,375	5.1
6	Georgia	8,919	4.0
7	Washington	7,733	3.5
8	Oklahoma	6,612	3.0
9	Ohio	6,141	2.8
10	South Carolina	6,007	2.7
11	Arizona	5,682	2.5
12	Alabama	5,564	2.5
13	Pennsylvania	5,414	2.4
14	Michigan	4,547	2.1
15	Indiana	4,500	2.0
16	Tennessee	4,481	2.0
17	Oregon	4,347	2.0
18	Kentucky	4,196	1.9
19	Virginia	4,158	1.9
20	Mississippi	4,002	1.8
21	Missouri	3,498	1.6
22	New York	3,228	1.5
23	Illinois	3,204	1.4
24	West Virginia	3,293	1.4
25	Colorado	2,890	1.3
26	New Mexico	2,699	1.2
27	Arkansas	2,533	1.1
28	Kansas	2,368	1.1
29	Wyoming	2,143	1.0
30	Wisconsin	2,033	0.9
31	Nevada	1,758	0.8
32	Iowa	1,744	0.8
33	Idaho	1,656	0.7
34	Minnesota	1,558	0.7
35	Montana	1,463	0.7
36	North Dakota	1,197	0.5
37	Utah	1,164	0.5
38	Maryland	1,148	0.5
39	Delaware	1,105	0.5
40	Nebraska	968	0.4
41	Maine	854	0.4

Table 4–18 (cont.)

Rank	State	Shipments	Percent of Total
42	New Hampshire	730	0.3
43	New Jersey	715	0.3
44	South Dakota	667	0.3
45	Massachusetts	523	0.2
46	Vermont	432	0.2
47	Connecticut	317	0.1
48	Alaska	114	0.1
49	Rhode Island	64	0.0
50	D.C. and U.S. Terr.	36	0.0
51	Hawaii	0	0.0

SOURCE: NCSBCS, MH Series.

Note: Percentages do not total 100 due to rounding.

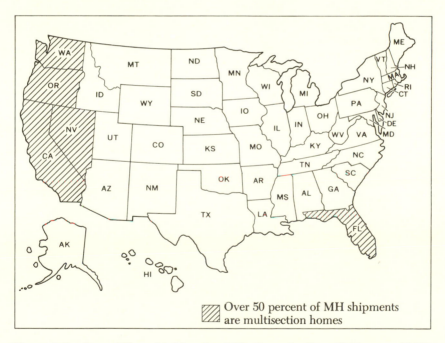

Figure 4–3 States Where Multisection MHs Comprise Over 50 Percent of MH Shipments, 1977–1980. Note: Oregon and Washington are 1978–1980 only. *(Source: Based on NCSBCS MH Series data.)*

Table 4–19   MH Units per 100,000 Population by State, 1980

Rank	State	MH Units/ 100,000 Population	Rank	State	MH Units/ 100,000 Population
1	Wyoming	4,173	26	Oklahoma	2,044
2	Arizona	4,022	27	Tennessee	2,012
3	Montana	4,021	28	Colorado	1,966
4	Nevada	3,950	29	New Hampshire	1,902
5	Idaho	3,838	30	Indiana	1,887
6	New Mexico	3,714	31	Texas	1,886
7	Florida	3,494	32	Missouri	1,700
8	South Carolina	3,386	33	Nebraska	1,629
9	North Carolina	3,340	34	Virginia	1,567
10	Alaska	3,205	35	Utah	1,468
11	Oregon	3,192	36	Michigan	1,444
12	Delaware	3,072	37	Minnesota	1,399
13	North Dakota	2,962	38	Iowa	1,298
14	West Virginia	2,884	39	Ohio	1,244
15	Georgia	2,846	40	Pennsylvania	1,237
16	Mississippi	2,825	41	California	1,226
17	Alabama	2,796	42	Wisconsin	1,132
18	South Dakota	2,767	43	Illinois	890
19	Washington	2,465	44	Maryland	614
20	Arkansas	2,458	45	New York	563
21	Louisiana	2,452	46	Connecticut	304
22	Kentucky	2,329	47	Rhode Island	279
23	Maine	2,306	48	New Jersey	267
24	Vermont	2,100	49	Massachusetts	229
25	Kansas	2,052	50	Hawaii	21

SOURCE: 1980 Census of Population and Housing, PHC80-V-1, April 1981, Advance Reports. Number of units derived from Table 4–12, this volume.

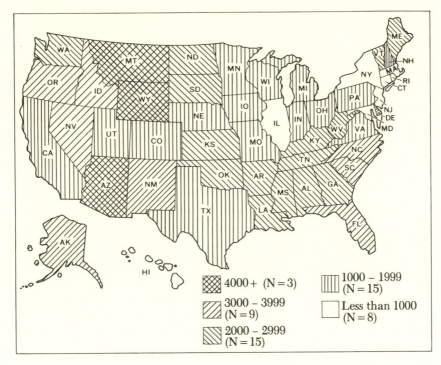

Figure 4–4   MH Units per 100,000 Population by State, 1980.

Consumer Issues

Two consumer issues are peculiar to this form of housing. The first is concerned with the guarantee of structural quality, the second with the unique legal and functional relationships between MH unit and MH park owners.

Structural Quality

Because MHs are often constructed, sited, and sold by three different parties, and because the structural type and means of transportation to site place particular demands on the structural integrity of MH units, a number of different guarantees relate to house quality. For the past several years the Federal Trade Commission (FTC) has been actively involved in a rule-making procedure pertinent to guaranteeing house quality. (This effort is described in some detail in Chapter 6.) The FTC's activity has been aimed at clearly identifying consumer rights and specifying accountability on the part of the traditional parties to the industry —manufacturer, transporter, and dealer. While industry trade groups first supported such a proceeding, they have subsequently opposed FTC intervention on the grounds that the HUD Code and complaint procedure provides sufficient safeguards, especially in those states with specific warranty statutes for MHs. However, early in the FTC process several of the major manufacturers did sign consent decrees with the FTC to establish their responsibilities for home quality.

In addition to manufacturer responsibility, several private corporations are providing home warranty services through dealers, with costs incorporated in the sales price of the home. The programs as advertised parallel home owner warranty (HOW) programs offered by site builders. Providing coverage for up to ten years, the programs guarantee structure and major home components (plumbing, heating, air conditioning, electrical, and so on). The warranty on a new MH will stay with the home throughout the term of coverage, regardless of owner. Furthermore, some companies are offering warranty coverage on existing MHs.

MH Unit and Park Owner Relationship

A second consumer issue peculiar to MHs is the set of legal and functional relationships found when an MH unit is located in an MH park. The difference in property status—the land owner holding real property and the MH owner holding personal property—has led to a presumption of legal priority for the land owner. This priority was important in an earlier era, when "trailer" owners indeed moved frequently, taking their homes with them. As MHs have become functionally immobile, however, equivalent changes to balance legal rights have not occurred. The owners of MHs in parks, especially those owning relatively newer homes, have a financial interest that, taken in aggregate, exceed that of the park owner, often by a large margin. Nevertheless, with certain (and increasingly frequent) exceptions, the unit owner's property rights continue to be subordinate to those of the park owner. Many parks still have only a tenant-at-will provision for

space occupancy, and many more have only short-term leases, in the one- to three-year range.

The park rules, determined by the park owner, have only recently come under public scrutiny, prompted by resident complaints of unreasonableness. The most typical complaint is that such rules place an unreasonable economic burden on owners at entry, in remaining, or in finding another location if evicted. The FTC has found that "closed" parks (parks in which entry is dependent on purchasing the MH unit from the park owner-dealer or from a designated dealer) are a violation of its rules. It recently entered into three consent orders with MH park owners relative to this practice. Some states have enacted statutes covering permissible activities for park operators. Most focus on establishing a standard of reasonableness for park rules and limiting the financial constraints a park owner may place on a resident. Some states have statutes enabling localities to impose rent controls on MH parks.

While states are addressing the problem of park and unit owner relations when a park is operative, they have not addressed the problem of property rights when a park owner decides to sell the park. In situations in which the park use will be continued, the costs for continued occupancy may rise substantially. In cases in which the use is to be changed (most frequently occurring in older parks located in commercially zoned areas) the unit owners are forced to move. In both situations the unit value associated with location (site and improvements) is lost. In the case of units located in older parks, the unit value may also be lost if it has deteriorated to the point that it will not withstand the rigors of transportation. Although, in some instances park residents have purchased the park on a condominium or cooperative basis, more frequently they are unable to assemble adequate financing.

Consumer Perceptions

MHs are unique in the singularity of image they evoke for consumers. Regardless of contemporary appearance and construction quality, the conventional image of an MH is that of a "mobile home" or, put more directly, a "trailer"—the pink and white rectangular box squeezed into a trailer park by the side of a highway, next to the aquamarine dinosaur in the miniature golf course. The

connotations are decidedly negative—structurally, aesthetically, socially, and culturally. The basic conclusion is that MHs are second-rate housing for second-class people.

The 1978 Owens-Corning study referred to earlier provided very definitive evidence of the continuation of this prevalent set of consumer perceptions. It also revealed that MH owners do not hold these perceptions, whereas they do tend to retain a distinction of some sort between MHs and "real" housing. The study summarized the elements of this perception as nine barriers to acceptance of MHs as "real" housing:

1. Low-quality materials and insufficient inspection of workmanship;
2. Unsafe/unsturdy;
3. Small in size, with small storage areas and limited provision for individual privacy;
4. Energy inefficient, with insufficient insulation and high heating and cooling costs;
5. Not a permanent residence;
6. The name "mobile home" being unacceptable in its implications;
7. Depreciation in value;
8. Location in unacceptable neighborhoods;
9. Inadequate financing.

The Owens-Corning study concluded that the first six barriers were solely perceptual, not supportable by contemporary evidence. Barriers 7 and 8 were found to be both real and perceptual, as some MHs appreciate or are located in acceptable areas. Barrier 9 was real, though financing advances since the study's completion would probably lead the analysts to classify it also as both real and perceptual.

Notes

1. A further difficulty is that vacant units are not counted as part of the stock, even if they are on the sales or rental market. Similarly, units for vacation or recreational use are not counted. Further, the AHS also does not count MHs on sites of ten or more acres. The 1976 AHS noted problems in the listing procedures used for finding MHs placed outside of parks.

2. The Owens-Corning study was done by the Opinion Research Corporation using a telephone interview method. Again, because the nature of home unit was self-reported, with "single-family house" being the first option, it is likely that the data are biased to some extent, with respondents self-reporting as SFDs units that strictly speaking are MHs.

3. Unless otherwise noted, cost estimates cited here are provided by the Manufactured Housing Institute.

4. In some instances the sales price may include furnishings, although this is a decreasing practice.

5. Bernhardt (1980, p. 268) reports MH park construction costs in 1977 ranging from $700 to $68,000 per space. A 150-space park near Washington, D.C., cost $7,000 per space, without community facilities. Deleting optional features—such as curbs and gutters, walks, a gas or oil system, street lights, storm drains, trees and shrubs, patios with privacy fencing, and pads for storage sheds—would drop the cost to $4,500 per space. These figures exclude transportation cost.

6. Cost estimates on transportation and set-up provided by Burt Chamberlain of Chamberlain Mobilehome Transport, Inc., of Thomaston, Connecticut.

7. Many MH parks provide considerably more than the minimum, with costs commensurate with units, services, and amenities. An example is Pinehurst Village in Plymouth, Massachusetts, where a two-bedroom unit sells in the $35,000 range, with monthly site rental for a 7,200 square foot lot and state in-lieu tax totaling about $110.00. The purchase price includes transportation and setup, landscaping, a covered porch, a cement patio, a 6 foot by 12 foot storage shed, and a two-car parking apron. The park has a large recreation hall, swimming pool, and tennis courts. All utilities are underground, with rubbish and garbage collected at the rear of units along a service road.

   An emerging variation on the traditional MH park is the condominium. One example is Harbor Isles in Venice, Florida. Similar in appearance to an MH park, the condominium provides land ownership and IRS tax benefits to resident owners. The condominium corporation owns and operates the development. Harbor Isles provides fully landscaped lots beginning at about 5,000 square feet. The sale price includes home and lot, with prices ranging from $35,000 to $54,000. Units are centrally heated and air conditioned, with a carport, driveway, and screened porch or Florida room. The community has a variety of recreational services, including swimming pool, recreation building, and tennis courts.

8. The trend is dramatic for multisectional MHs. In 1975 only 10.1 percent of reporting financial institutions used a simple interest method, with an additional 8.9 percent using both simple and add-on interest methods. By 1980 the proportion using simple interest had risen to 41.4 percent, with an additional 7.5 percent using both methods. In 1980 59.6 percent of reporting S&Ls used the simple interest method (MHI, 1976; 1981*b*).

9. It should be noted that reporting institutions in the MHI survey may use several of the possible portfolio protection methods.
10. For example, Foremost found that a significant factor in determining into which group a state was assigned was the availability of MH park space and/or the degree of restrictive zoning (Malnight, p. 24).

Chapter 5

THE STATES AND
MANUFACTURED HOMES

The use of any given housing form in a particular market is the result of a number of different factors. For most analysts the two dominant factors are price, including the cost and availability of financing, and consumer preference. For housing forms seen within the range of conventional choice, these two factors are undoubtedly dominant. For housing forms somehow labeled "unconventional," however, other factors are more critical. Because of their structural distinctiveness and unique evolution as a housing choice, manufactured homes have received unique treatment in housing markets. Earlier chapters described many of the attributes of this housing and the process by which it reaches its markets, with the focus primarily on private sector aspects. In this chapter and in Chapter 6 the public sector treatment of MHs is discussed.

Public sector actions and attitudes provide an envelope within which housing markets operate; government both initiates and regulates market activities. Public sector policies can encourage or discourage certain kinds of housing activities; government programs serve as incentives to adopt certain kinds of housing solutions, and as barriers to others. Finally, public regulations explicitly channel the nature and location of acceptable housing activities.

This chapter considers public sector actions and attitudes at the state and local levels.[1] It summarizes for the 50 states and the District of Columbia the status of manufactured homes in terms of formal housing policy, implementing programs, financing through state housing finance agencies, tax status, and form of ownership recording and development controls, whether statutory or through legal precedent.

MHs and State Housing Policy

State housing policy, where it exists formally, tends to be prepared by the state's planning office (or an equivalently central staff agency or division) and to be adopted by executive order, by vote of the legislature or an appointive policy body such as a state planning council. State planning is often undertaken on a comprehensive basis, frequently with assistance from HUD's comprehensive planning assistance program. In such cases housing becomes one of several elements of an overall state plan, which would include a statement of policy (general and topic-specific), proposed implementation programs, and an analysis in support of both policy and programs. State planning may also be topic-specific, prepared by a functional agency such as a department of economic development. Such planning may or may not involve federal funds and may or may not be comprehensive in its considerations.

The states exhibit a wide range of housing policy activity (Table 5–1). A surprising number of states (15) report no formal housing policy; of the 36 with a formal housing policy, only 17 report that the policy mentions MHs in any way (see Table 5–2).

As shown in Figure 5–1, there are some interesting geographic clusterings in terms of policy status. Most western states tend to have a housing policy mentioning MHs. (Although California does not mention MH explicitly, the state has many MH programs, and recent major policy shifts on tax status give this state a de facto MH policy.) States with considerable MH activity tend to have a housing policy mentioning MH, whether that activity was in absolute numbers (for example, Texas) or relative to the scale of the housing market (for example, Nebraska). Many of the states with high MH activity also anticipate changes, a reflection of the continuing importance of this housing form for these states. The only geographic clustering of "change" states is the Northeast. Six of the nine states anticipate change, perhaps reflecting the possible

Table 5–1   MH and State Housing Policy

State	Policy	Adopting Entity	MH Addressed	Change
AL	Yes	Office of State Planning Federal Programs	No	No
AK	Yes	In preparation	No	No
AZ	Yes	Governor; prepared by the Office of Economic Planning and Development	Yes	No
AR	No		No	No
CA	Yes	Department of Housing and Community Development	No	Yes
CO	No	In preparation	No	Yes
CT	Yes	General Assembly	No	Yes
DC	No		No	No
DE	Yes	Legislature	No	Yes
FL	Yes	Department of Housing and Community Development; Governor	Yes	Yes
GA	Yes	Department of Community Affairs	No	Yes
HI	Yes	Draft prepared for legislative action	No	No
ID	Yes	Legislature	Yes	No
IL	Yes	Governor	No	No
IN	Yes	State Planning Services Agency	No	No
IO	Yes	Office for Planning and Programming	Yes	No
KS	No	Kansas Department of Economic Development	No	Yes
KY	No		No	No
LA	No	Local level	No	No
ME	Yes	Governor and MH Board	No	No
MD	Yes	Governor	No	No
MA	Yes	Executive Office of Communities and Development	Yes	Yes
MI	Yes	Legislature	No	No
MN	Yes	State Planning Office and Office of Local and Urban Affairs	Yes	No
MS	No	Division of Housing Coordination	No	No
MO	No	Housing Development; Commission created by the Legislature	No	No
MT	No	Housing Act of '75 establishing financial assistance	No	No
NE	Yes	Division of Community Affairs	Yes	No
NV	Yes	Governor's Office of Planning Coordination	No	Yes
NH	Yes	Governor's Advisory Commission	Yes	Yes
NJ	No		No	Yes
NM	Yes	State Housing and Rural Development Authority	No	No

Table 5–1 (cont.)

State	Policy	Adopting Entity	MH Addressed	Change
NY	Yes	Division of Planning and Federal Assistance	Yes	No
NC	Yes	Division of Community Housing	Yes	No
ND	Yes	State Planning Division	No	Yes
OH	Yes	Governor's office	No	No
OK	No	In preparation, Department of Economic and Community Affairs	No	Yes
OR	Yes	Legislature	Yes	No
PA	No	In preparation	No	Yes
RI	Yes	State Planning Council	Yes	No
SC	No	Housing Authority	No	No
SD	Yes	Legislature	No	No
TN	Yes	Tennessee Housing Development Agency and Tennessee State Planning Office	No	No
TX	Yes	Office of Governor	Yes	Yes
UT	Yes	Legislature	Yes	No
VT	Yes	Department of Housing and Community Affairs	Yes	Yes
VA	No		No	No
WA	Yes	Governor	Yes	Yes
WV	No	Governor's Office of Economic and Community Development	No	Yes
WI	Yes	Housing Division, Department of Local Affairs and Development	No	Yes
WY	Yes	State Planning Office	Yes	No

SOURCE: Nutt-Powell, Thomas E., and Michael Furlong, with Christopher Pilkington. 1980. *The States and Manufactured Housing.* Cambridge, Mass.: Joint Center for Urban Studies, pp. 4–6.

Table 5–2 Number of States with Formal Housing Policy, Mention of MH, Change Anticipated, May 1980

	Yes	No
Formal housing policy	36	15
Mention of MH	17	34
Change anticipated	20	31

SOURCE: Nutt-Powell, Thomas E., and Michael Furlong, with Christopher Pilkington. 1980. *The States and Manufactured Housing.* Cambridge, Mass.: Joint Center for Urban Studies, p. 7.

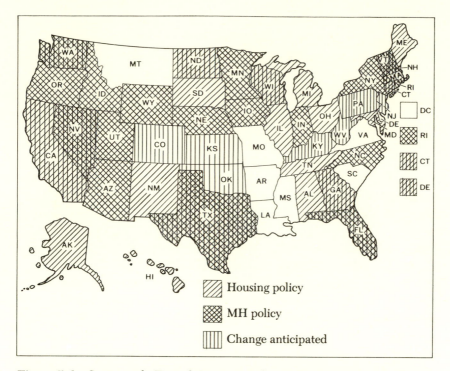

Figure 5–1   States with Formal Housing Policy, MH Mention, and Change Anticipated, May 1980. *(Source: Nutt-Powell, Thomas E., and Michael Furlong with Christopher Pilkington. 1980. The States and Manufactured Housing. Cambridge, Mass.: Joint Center for Urban Studies, p. 3.)*

consideration of this little-used housing form to respond to high housing purchase and operating costs in this region.

Apparently the failure to mention MH in formal housing policy is based on an ignorance of MHs on the part of housing planners and policymakers. This ignorance persists in part because of an unconscious bias in favor of site-built housing, a bias supported by daily encounter with this housing form. In general not only does housing policy not mention manufactured homes, few mention *any* form of manufactured housing. In most respects, it is fair to characterize planners' view of housing as very conventional, with little imagination about alternative structural solutions to meet desired housing objectives.

This view is reinforced by instances in which MHs have been included in a state's housing policy as the result of an encounter with this housing form. For example, while Massachusetts' housing policy published in June 1978 made no reference to MHs, an update issued one year later included discussion of MH as a housing form as well as a potential contributor to the state's economic development. This discussion was prompted by the work of the state's Mobile Homes Commission on the role of the MH in meeting state housing needs, work reviewed by the state's Office of Policy Development and used in its preparation of housing policy.

Although many states either have no housing policy or do not mention MHs, many (20) report that they expect a change in that situation. Some states report circumstances similar to Massachusetts, where current policy deliberations are likely to yield policy shifts. A good example is New Jersey, where the legislature created a Mobile Homes Study Commission. The commission, consisting of representatives of the legislature, state agencies, and the MH industry, has broad powers to review the status and potential role of the MH in the state's housing market. It is anticipated that the work of the commission will lead to changes in state and local policy, legislation, and programs.[2]

A second group of states has long recognized the importance of MHs in their housing markets. Over time these states have developed policies pertinent to the use of this housing form, and a considerable amount of policy is now embedded in statute and administrative guidelines. For example, Florida, as part of its Local Government Comprehensive Planning Act (1975), provides that MHs be treated as any other development under the act, except that the housing element of each jurisdiction must make provisions for sites for MHs. The implications of this policy are important given that housing elements, when adopted, have the legal effect of an ordinance. Similarly, Florida's Building Construction Standards provide that local requirements and regulations "must be reasonable and uniformly applied and enforced without distinctions as to whether such housing is factory-built or built in a conventional manner."

State MH Programs

States have a variety of housing policy implementation mechanisms available, from information assembly to technical assistance to direct funding and/or implementation of programs of a community development nature. In understanding public sector attitudes and actions, a first area of interest is the extent of knowledge of state agencies of either regulatory or direct assistance mechanisms pertaining to MHs. A second area is the content of such mechanisms.

State governments exhibit a surprising lack of knowledge about regulatory and/or assistance mechanisms, matched by an absence of MH programs (see Table 5–3). Twenty-five states report an absence of information on both local zoning practices *and* guiding

Table 5–3   **MH Land Use Controls Knowledge and MH Program Existence in States**

State	State Level Knowledge of:			State MH Programs	Changes in State MH Programs Anticipated
	MH Land Use Statute Reference	MH Land Use Controls Court Decisions	Local MH Zoning Practices		
AL	N	N	N	N	N
AK	N	N	N	Y	Y
AZ	N	Y	Y	N	N
AR	N	N	N	N	N
CA	Y	N	Y	Y	Y
CO	N	Y	N	Y	N
CT	N	N	N	N	N
DE	N	N	N	Y	N
DC	N	N	N	N	N
FL	Y	Y	N	Y	N
GA	N	N	N	N	N
HI	N	N	N	N	N
ID	N	N	Y	N	N
IL	N	N	N	N	N
IN	N	Y	Y	Y	Y
IO	N	Y	N	Y	N
KS	N	N	N	N	N
KY	N	N	N	N	N
LA	N	Y	N	N	Y
ME	N	Y	Y	N	N
MD	N	N	Y	N	N
MA	Y	Y	Y	N	Y
MI	N	Y	Y	Y	N
MN	N	N	Y	Y	N
MS	N	N	Y	N	N
MO	N	N	N	N	N

Table 5–3 (cont.)

State	State Level Knowledge of:				
	MH Land Use Statute Reference	*MH Land Use Controls Court Decisions*	*Local MH Zoning Practices*	*State MH Programs*	*Changes in State MH Programs Anticipated*
MT	N	Y	Y	Y	Y
NE	Y	Y	N	N	Y
NV	N	N	N	Y	Y
NH	N	Y	N	N	Y
NJ	N	Y	N	N	Y
NM	N	N	N	N	N
NY	N	Y	Y	N	N
NC	N	N	N	N	Y
ND	N	N	N	N	N
OH	N	N	N	N	N
OK	N	N	N	N	Y
OR	Y	Y	Y	Y	N
PA	Y	Y	N	Y	N
RI	N	N	Y	N	N
SC	N	N	N	N	Y
SD	N	N	N	Y	N
TN	N	N	N	Y	N
TX	N	Y	Y	N	Y
UT	N	N	N	N	N
VT	Y	N	Y	N	Y
VA	N	N	N	N	N
WA	N	Y	N	Y	Y
WV	N	N	N	Y	Y
WI	Y	Y	Y	Y	Y
WY	N	N	N	N	N

Source: Nutt-Powell, Thomas E., and Michael Furlong, with Christopher Pilkington. 1980. *The States and Manufactured Housing.* Cambridge, Mass.: Joint Center for Urban Studies, pp. 13–14.

Y = yes.
N = no.

court cases on regulating use of MHs (see Table 5–4). Southeastern states represent a large number of this group, whereas west coast and northeastern states tend to be among those with knowledge of zoning and/or court cases (see Figure 5–2). The number of states with both knowledge of zoning practices *and* of guiding court decisions was small, only 10 (see Table 5–4). Thus it is not surprising that few states report much in the way of technical assistance activities aimed at assisting localities to for-

Table 5–4 Number of States with MH Zoning and/or Court Case Knowledge

	Yes	*No*
Zoning	17	34
Court case	19	32
Both	10	41
Neither	25	26

SOURCE: Nutt-Powell, Thomas E., and Michael Furlong, with Christopher Pilkington. 1980. *The States and Manufactured Housing.* Cambridge, Mass.: Joint Center for Urban Studies, p. 14.

mulate sound planning and regulatory approaches to MH use in local housing situations.

Oregon is a good example of a state providing active guidance. Its statewide housing goal, known as Goal 10, is implemented by a requirement that each jurisdiction inventory buildable lands. This inventory is then cross-referenced with plan and zoning

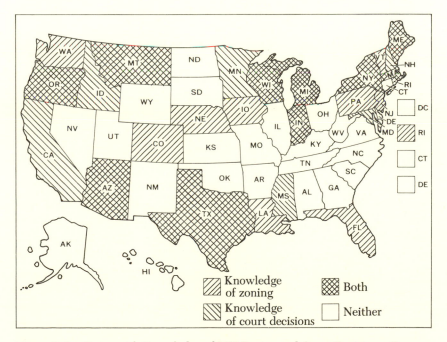

Figure 5–2 States with Knowledge of MH Zoning and Court Decisions. (*Source: Nutt-Powell, Thomas E., and Michael Furlong with Christopher Pilkington. 1980. The States and Manufactured Housing. Cambridge, Mass.: Joint Center for Urban Studies, p. 15.*)

Table 5–5   Number of States with MH Programs and/or Change Anticipated

	Yes	No
MH programs	18	33
Change anticipated	18	33
Both	8	43
Neither	23	28

SOURCE: Nutt-Powell, Thomas E., and Michael Furlong, with Christopher Pilkington. 1980. *The States and Manufactured Housing.* Cambridge, Mass.: Joint Center for Urban Studies, p. 17.

designations to ensure available land for all residential categories. A state decision on the comprehensive plan for the city of St. Helens limits the application of discretionary criteria, especially for MHs. This decision, distributed to other jurisdictions, serves as guidance in formulation of local plans in conformance with Goal 10.

In a similar manner, California requires that local jurisdictions prepare local housing elements with local plans that provide a "fair-share allocation" in meeting the full spectrum of market area housing needs. The state's Department of Housing and Community Development reviews these plans and has powers to curtail local development until it proceeds in accordance with a plan acceptable to the agency. This review has been applied primarily to encourage lower cost housing and has resulted in the development of MH communities as one mechanism for meeting housing needs.

Only 18 states have MH programs (see Table 5–5 and Figure 5–3); of these, 8 anticipate change. Ten states not having MH programs anticipate some change in the situation; 23 states have no program and anticipate no change. Many states have an MH Commission, either permanent or special. Some states use special state funds for construction purposes—for example, Delaware aided in the development of a model MH park in 1976. Some states have allocated state-controlled Section 8 housing assistance funds for MH purposes; others have state technical-assistance programs aimed at innovative use of MHs. Many of the more ambitious state programs (reported in the next section) involve use of state financing powers.

States anticipate change in both regulatory and direct-assistance

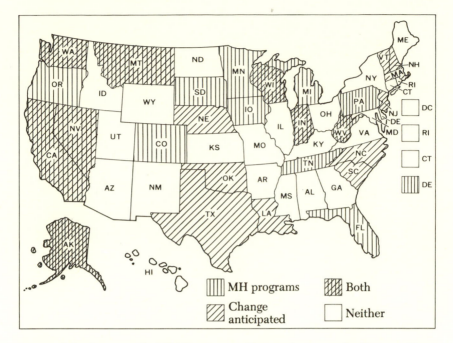

Figure 5-3   States with MH Programs, Change Anticipated. *(Source: Nutt-Powell, Thomas E., and Michael Furlong with Christopher Pilkington. 1980. The States and Manufactured Housing. Cambridge, Mass.: Joint Center for Urban Studies, p. 18.)*

activities. For example, New Jersey anticipates a wide range of changes, including tax status, zoning guidance, and overall policy as a result of its study commission. Washington anticipates promoting use of solar technologies in MHs and use of MHs to meet rising housing demands brought about by economic expansion.

Housing Finance Agencies and MHs

Housing finance agencies (HFAs) use the tax-free status of publicly issued bonds to create a source of funds for housing at an interest rate lower than prevailing market rates. Most HFAs issue revenue bonds, which link repayment to monthly loan payments from the housing developed and/or rehabilitated using funds obtained from the bond sale.

Housing finance agencies exist in 43 states (see Figure 5-4) and have a varying impact on a state's housing market. Most HFAs

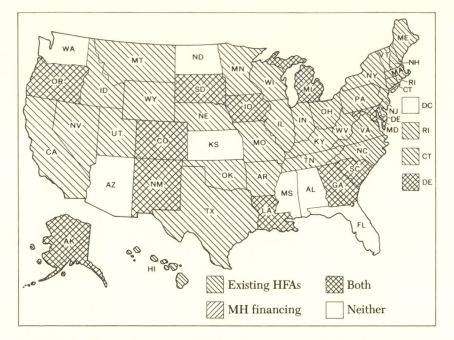

Figure 5–4 States with Housing Finance Agencies and MH Financing. *(Source: Nutt-Powell, Thomas E., and Michael Furlong with Christopher Pilkington. 1980. The States and Manufactured Housing. Cambridge, Mass.: Joint Center for Urban Studies, p. 28.)*

provide funding for both single-family and multifamily housing for rental and owner use (Table 5–6). Some have additional programs such as funding housing rehabilitation. Only 14 HFAs are or are about to be involved in MH financing (see Table 5–7). The extent of involvement in most cases represents a small proportion of the agency's activity, from a minimum of one unit (Colorado) to a special bond issue for MHs (Alaska) to a continuing and rather extensive funding through a state-created program for veterans (Oregon).

Although 14 HFAs have some MH financing, most exhibit almost complete ignorance of MHs. Some HFAs clearly are not aware of the distinction between MHs and other forms of manufactured housing and, in effect, disregard all as forms of housing to be considered. Many agencies with authorization to finance MHS have chosen to not use this power.

Of the HFAs participating in MH financing, Georgia and Oregon are illustrative of two relatively distinct approaches. The Georgia Residential Finance Authority, which makes direct loans,

Table 5–6 Housing Finance Agency Activity

State	Agency	Coverage*				MH Status**		
		SF	MFD	Rent	Own	Auth.	Guide	# MH Financed
AL	None							
AK	AK Housing Finance Corp. and	Y	Y	Y	Y	Y	Y	None
	Mobile Home Loan Program	Y	N	N	Y	Y	Y	Just underway
AZ	None							
AR	AR Housing Development Agency	Y	Y	Y	Y	N	N	None
CA	CA Housing Finance Agency	Y	Y	Y	Y	N	N	None
CO	CO Housing Finance Agency	Y	Y	Y	Y	N	Y	
CT	CT Housing Finance Authority	Y	Y	Y	Y	N	N	None
DE	DE State Housing Authority, and	Y	Y	Y	Y	N	N	None
	DE Housing Development Fund	Y	Y	N	Y	Y	Y	Has financed a 39-Unit MH Park
DC	None							
FL	None							
GA	GA Residential Finance Authority	Y	Y	Y	Y	N	N	Secondary market FHA and VA paper purchased
HI	HI Housing Authority	Y	Y	Y	Y	N	N	None
ID	ID Housing Agency	Y	Y	Y	Y	N	N	None
IL	IL Housing Development Authority	N	Y	Y	N	N	N	None
IN	IN Housing Finance Authority	Y	Y	Y	Y	N	N	None
IO	IO Housing Finance Authority	Y	Y	Y	Y	N	N	Some

Table 5–6 (cont.)

State	Agency	Coverage*					MH Status**	
		SF	MFD	Rent	Own	Auth.	Guide	# MH Financed
KS	None							
KY	KY Housing Corporation	Y	Y	Y	Y	N	N	None
LA	Local HFAs	Y	N	N	Y	Y	Y	Yes, in at least one local HFA
ME	ME State Housing Authority	Y	Y	Y	Y	Y	N	None
MD	Community Development Administration	Y	Y	Y	Y	N	Y	Yes (MH comprise 7% of all homes financed)
MA	MA Housing Finance Agency, and MA Home Mortgage Finance Agency	N	Y	Y	N	N	N	None
MI	MI State Housing Development Authority	Y	Y	Y	Y	Y	N	None
MN	MN Housing Finance Authority	Y	Y	Y	Y	N	Y	Some
MS	None							
MO	MO Housing Development Commission	Y	Y	Y	Y	N	Y	None
MT	MT Board of Housing	Y	Y	Y	Y	N	N	None
NE	NE Mortgage Finance Fund	Y	N	N	Y	N	N	None
NV	NV Housing Division	Y	Y	Y	Y	N	Y	None
NH	NH Housing Finance Agency	Y	Y	Y	Y	N	N	None
NJ	NJ Housing Finance Agency	N	Y	Y	N	N	N	None
NM	NM Mortgage Finance Authority	Y	N	N	Y	Y	Y	Less than 100
NY	NY State Housing Finance Agency	N	Y	Y	N	N	N	None
NC	NC State Housing Finance Agency	Y	Y	Y	Y	N	N	None
ND	None							
OH	OH Housing Development Board	N	Y	Y	N	N	N	None
OK	OK Housing Finance Agency	N	Y	Y	N	N	N	None

State	Agency	SF	MFD	Rent	Own	Auth.	Guide	Number
OR	Housing Division Department of Commerce, and	Y	Y	Y	Y	Y	Y	23
	Department of Veterans Affairs	Y	Y	Y	Y	Y	Y	2,212 in 1979
PA	PA Housing Finance Agency	N	N	Y	N	N	N	None
RI	RI Housing and Mortgage Finance Corporation	Y	Y	Y	Y	Y	Y	None
SC	SC State Housing Authority	Y	Y	Y	Y	Y	Y	Yes
SD	SD Housing Development Authority	Y	Y	Y	Y	Y	Y	Less than 50
TN	TN Housing Development Agency	Y	Y	Y	Y	Y	N	None
TX	TX Housing Finance Agency	Y	Y	Y	Y	Y	N	None
UT	UT Housing Finance Agency	Y	Y	Y	Y	Y	N	None
VT	VT Housing Finance Authority	Y	Y	Y	Y	Y	Y	30
VA	VA Housing Development Authority	Y	Y	Y	Y	Y	N	500
WA	None							
WV	WVA Housing Development Fund	Y	Y	Y	Y	Y	N	None
WI	WI Housing Finance Authority	N	Y	Y	Y	Y	N	None
WY	WY Community Development Agency	Y	N	N	Y	Y	N	None

SOURCE: Nutt-Powell, Thomas E., and Michael Furlong, with Christopher Pilkington. 1980. *The States and Manufactured Housing*. Cambridge, Mass.: Joint Center for Urban Studies, pp. 21–27.

* Has type of coverage:
    SF = Single-family
    MFD = Multifamily dwelling
    Rent = Rental
    Own = Ownership

** MH status:
    Auth. = Is there an agency with authorization to finance MHs?
    Guide = Is there a guide for MH financing?

Y = yes.
N = no.

Table 5–7   Housing Finance Agency Existence and MH Financing

	Yes	*No*
HFA	43	8
MH financing	14	37

SOURCE: Nutt-Powell, Thomas E., and Michael Furlong with Christopher Pilking-ton. 1980. *The States and Manufactured Housing.* Cambridge, Mass.: Joint Center for Urban Studies, p. 29.

also participates in the secondary mortgage market, buying FHA and VA paper. Since both these agencies have MH programs, the participation of the GRFA increases the availability of funds for MHs. By comparison, Oregon's Department of Veteran Affairs housing bond program has a long-standing and very active MH loan program. Interest rates and down payments vary depending on whether the loan is on the unit only or the land and unit together. A total of 2,212 loans were made through this program in 1979.

Taxation of MHs

Historically, MHs have been classified as personal property for taxation purposes, a practice derived from the initial size and mobility of mobile homes. As the size of MHs has increased, the states have begun to adjust the tax classification. With the dramatic increase in proportion of multisection MH units over the past few years, and the even more dramatic drop in mobility (other than the initial move from plant to site), the variations in tax classification from state to state are more pronounced.

MHs have a tax classification for both property and sales tax purposes; Table 5–8 presents a summary of tax status for both purposes. The remainder of this section discusses first property, then sales tax status.

Table 5–8 Taxation of MHs

State	Property Tax		In Lieu	Sales Tax	
	Personal	Real		Original Sale	Subsequent Sale
AL	If not affixed (20% FMV, 10% if owner-occupied)	If affixed*		1.5% state** plus registration	Vendor only
AK	If not affixed	If affixed*		0%–6% local, varies (median, 3%, 1978)	
AZ	If single-section *and* if not affixed	If multisection *and* If affixed* (from 1979)	Until 1978	4% state + local (on 60% of price)	None
AR	If not affixed	If affixed		3% state** + local	None
CA		If purchased after July '80	Before July 1980	6%–6.5% state and local; based on 60% if affixed & on 80% if not	Same
CO	If not affixed (30% of value)	If affixed		3% State; 0.5% local option; on 52% of price	None
CT	If not affixed	If affixed*		7% State; 7.5% July '80	Vendor or casual
DE	None (even if not affixed)	If affixed		2% document fee upon titling	2% retitling except if affixed
DC	Not applicable	Not applicable		None	None
FL	None	If affixed, choice: license or real property	License fee, by size	4% state** upon titling and register; $/size	Upon retitling or transfer of title; if affixed: deed tax

Table 5–8 (cont.)

State	Property Tax		In Lieu	Sales Tax	
	Personal	Real		Original Sale	Subsequent Sale
GA	If not affixed	If affixed*		3% state; 1% local (opt)	Vendor only; (transfer and recording tax if affixed)
HI		If affixed			
ID		All MHs		3% on 55% of purchase price	None
IL		If affixed	Privilege tax if not affixed	4% state; up to 2% local plus registration fee	Same, except if affixed
IN	If not affixed	If affixed		4% state	Vendor only
IO	If not affixed	If affixed		3% state plus registration fee	Vendor only
KS	If not affixed	If affixed*		3% state	Vendor and occasional
KY	If not affixed	If affixed	Excise tax on first registration	5% state	Vendor only
LA	None	If affixed		3% state** (titling) plus local tax	Upon retitling
ME		All MHs	Excise, if registered for road movement	5% state	None
MD	If not affixed	If affixed		5% state	5% upon retitle
MA	None	If affixed	Local $6–12/ month	5% state	Vendor only

State					
MI	None	If affixed	$3/mo for MH in parks	4% state	None
MN	If not affixed or affixed but land not owned	If affixed*		4% state	Vendor only
MS	If not affixed	If affixed*		3% state on home; 5% on furnishings	None
MO	If not affixed	If affixed		3⅛% state** plus local	Vendor
MT	If not affixed	If affixed*		None	None
NE	If not affixed or not on owned land	If affixed		3% state**; up to 1% municipal use	Vendor only
NV	If not affixed	If affixed* (from 7/1/79)		2% state, 1% school, .5% local	Vendor only
NH	If not affixed	If affixed*		None	None
NJ		All MH (from 1979)	(until 1979)	5% state	5% state if affixed
NM		All MHs		Gross receipts and compensating tax 3.75% state and up to .75% local (optional)	Only MHs initially sold before 4/79
NY		All MHs		4% state plus local (up to 8% total)	Vendor and casual
NC	All MHs			2% state** plus local	Vendor only
ND	None	If affixed*	"Decal" for all MHs, except if on farm	None	None

Table 5–8 (cont.)

State	Property Tax			Sales Tax	
	Personal	Real	In Lieu	Original Sale	Subsequent Sale
OH			Privilege tax	4% state plus local option	Vendor and casual
OK	None	If affixed	$25 plus $.75/100 of value in excess of $1500, devalued 5% annually	2% excise tax in lieu of sales tax	Vendor or retitle
OR	*Ad valorem* on 100% true cash value	If affixed*		None	None
PA	(varies by county)			A realty transfer tax of 1% (state) and 1% (local, optional) is collected at sale/resale of MH classified as real property; if unaffixed then MH is subject to 6% state sales tax on any original and subsequent sales	
RI	If not affixed	If affixed		6% state**	Vendor only
SC	None	All MHs; 4% of FMV if owned; 6% if leased		4% state**	Vendor only
SD	None	If affixed	Decal, based on full market value	3% registry	No sales tax, but 3% registry fee if retitled
TN	None	On 25% FMV		4.5% state plus local up to 6% total	Vendor or retitle

State	Taxed as personal property	Taxed as real property	Parking fee	Tax rate	Collected by
TX	If not affixed	If affixed		4% state; 1% local plus transit tax	Vendor/casual
UT		All MHs		4% state, 3/4% local, 1/4% selected counties	Vendor only
VT		All MH		Vendor/contractor; 3% state	Vendor only; 3% state
VA	All MH			3% upon titling	3% upon retitling
WA	If not affixed	If affixed		5.1% to 5.3% (4.3% state; .5% local; .1–3% transit)	1% excise tax
WV	If not affixed or if affixed on non-owned land	If affixed*		3% state or 3% use tax**	Vendor only
WI	If not parking fee and does not meet 50% test	If assessable value of attachments, foundations, etc. = or exceeds 50% of value of the unit	Monthly parking fee (some municipalities in MH parks)	4% state**	At time of registration
WY	If not affixed	If affixed*		Vendor 3% state + up to 1% county (optional); (on 60% of invoice)	Same (depreciated invoice base)

SOURCE: Nutt-Powell, Thomas E., and Michael Furlong, with Christopher Pilkington. 1980. *The States and Manufactured Housing.* Cambridge, Mass.: Joint Center for Urban Studies, pp. 34–38.

* On owner-occupied land.
** Use tax also.

Property Tax

Property can be classified for tax purposes in one of three ways: as real property, which connotes durability and permanence of location; as personal property, which implies portability; or in an *in lieu* category, which is item specific and provides a taxation method in lieu of either real or personal property taxation.

Most states continue to provide for the potential mobility of MHs by providing classification as either personal property or an in lieu status, even if they also provide a real property classification. Many of the in lieu classifications are linked with the MH park tradition. For example, Michigan provides that MHs installed in a licensed MH park pay a $3 monthly in lieu tax, collected by the park owner and remitted to the local jurisdiction. By comparison MHs installed on privately owned land "in such a manner as to become realty" are assessed as real property by the jurisdiction. Other states, such as Florida, assess an annual registration fee based on the size of the MH unit. A variation on the annual fee approach is used in Oklahoma, which bases the fee on the value of the unit by using a state-established depreciation schedule. Some in lieu categories also provide further special treatment. For example, North Dakota MH owners apply to the county director of tax equalization for a tax decal, and the tax assessment is based on a state-developed guide. However, MHs located on a farm and used as a farm residence are exempt from the tax decal provisions if permanently attached to the ground.

In general, the rule applied to classify MHs as real or personal property distinguishes whether the unit is "affixed" to the land on which it is sited. The definition of "affixed" varies, but in general the intent is to establish permanence. Some states have a further requirement that the land be owned by the MH owner; others further require that the unit be owner-occupied to achieve real property status. California recently enacted legislation to change MH tax status from an in lieu procedure to a real property classification, regardless of "affixation."[3] By comparison, Arizona makes a distinction between single- and multisection MHs in that only multisection MHs may be real property if affixed. In some states a different tax rate is applied within a category, based on occupancy. Alabama, for example, assesses MHs classed as personal property at 20 percent of fair market value, unless owner-occupied, in which case the assessment is 10 percent of fair market value. A number of states, such as California, have enacted legislation providing the real property classification. Others have changed classification as the result of court challenge, among them Nebraska and New Jersey.

Sales Tax

Most states levy a tax on the sale of MHs, generally a state tax, but also either a local tax or a local optional add-on to the state tax. While most such taxes apply only to sales within the state, others are also imposed on MHs purchased in another state for use in the taxing state. Many states tax only the original sale of the MH unit. In an effort to rectify unequal tax treatment between MHs and site-built homes, some states have recently established a tax basis other than the full sales price. This change reflects an attempt to avoid a tax on MH construction labor since only the materials are taxed on site-built homes. For example, Idaho provides for a 3 percent sales tax on 55 percent of the purchase price of an MH.

MH Ownership Recording

Because most states continue to have a personal property classification for at least some MHs, most have a formal procedure to publicly record the ownership (see Table 5–9). Most states issue a title, a practice based on the era of mobility when MHs and motor vehicles were sensibly linked together for administrative purposes. In most instances the nature of the title and the administering agency have not changed: Typically the state's department of motor vehicles issues and transfers titles and records liens. In general the titling practice has continued as a means of establishing ownership for lien recording purposes. Hence in states that have made the title optional, it is usually sought and issued in connection with obtaining a purchase loan.

Some states have no titling procedure. In some cases the legal status as real property means that the MH unit will be recorded on the deed as a property improvement, except for those cases in which the unit owner does not own land. New York is an example of such a state. If the state has no explicit provision for recording

Table 5–9 MH Ownership Recording Method

State	MH Method	MH Locus	State	MH Method	MH Locus
AL	Registration; no T	Department of Revenue MV and License Division	MA	none	
			MI	T	Mobile Home Commission, Department of Commerce
AK	T O	MVD/Department of Public Safety	MN	T	Division of Driver and Vehicle Services
AZ	T R	MVD/DOT			
AR	T	Revenue Office, Department of Finance and Administration	MS	Registration	County Tax Assessor
			MO	T	DMV
			MT	T O	RMV
			NE	T	DMV
CA	Registration; no T	DMV	NV	T	MHD
			NH	T	DMV
CO	T R	MVD	NJ	T R	DMV
CT	T O	DMV	NM	T	MVD
DE	T O	MVD	NY		
DC	T O	MVD	NC	T R	DMV
FL	T	Department of Highway Safety and MV	ND	T R	MVD
			OH	T R	DMV
			OK	T R	MVD
			OR	T	MVD
GA	T	DMV	PA	T O	DMV
HI	none		RI	T O	RMV
ID	T	MHD	SC	T	Department of Public Transportation and Highways
IL	T	Secretary of State			
IN	Bill of sale/deed	Local Government	SD	T	DMV
IO	T	DOT/OMV	TN	T O	MVD
KS	T	Vehicle Division, Revenue Department	TX	T	DMV
			UT	T	MVD
			VT	T O	DMV
KY	T/Registration	MV Tax Division/DOT	VA	T	DMV
			WA	T	Department of Licenses
LA	T	MVD, Department of Public Safety	WV	T O	DMV
			WI	T R	DMV
ME	none		WY	T O	Motor Vehicle Control Division
MD	T R	MV Administration			

SOURCE: Nutt-Powell, Thomas E., and Michael Furlong, with Christopher Pilkington. 1980. *The States and Manufactured Housing.* Cambridge, Mass.: Joint Center for Urban Studies, pp. 41–42.

T = Title   R = Required   O = Optional

as part of the deed or titling, the only mechanism to establish ownership is the bill of sale. Lenders wishing to record a lien will use the UCC–1 form and file it with the municipality's clerk. However, few mechanisms clearly establish a clear record of ownership from state to state in those instances in which the unit is moved on second or subsequent purchase.

MH Development Controls

As contrasted with the previous topics, development controls (as achieved through either statute or legal precedent)—are neither systematically devised nor regularly recorded. As noted in the earlier discussion of state programs, few states have knowledge of local development controls (zoning ordinances, health and building codes) and pertinent court cases guiding the application of development controls to MHs. Although some states, such as Florida and Oregon, are changing the nature of legislation enabling localities to apply development controls, these are the exceptions rather than the rule. Thus this section does not provide a systematic review of comparative evidence from a single (or relatively few) state agencies. Rather it is an assessment of reported court cases and new statutes for the time period 1970–1980.

It is important to reiterate that each state has a different approach to MH development control, and determination of the appropriateness of these controls varies in the courts. Moreover, adjoining states do not exhibit the similarity of decisions one finds for other housing issues, where regional characteristics tend to significantly influence local controls.

One reason for the variation among states and absence of trends is the relative paucity of laws and cases. Only 3 states had as many as 20 cases during the 10-year study period; most had fewer than 10 and many had none whatsoever. Given the number in existence at the beginning of the decade (1.85 million) and the number produced during the decade (approximately 3.6 million), MHs are clearly a considerable component of the housing stock. Moreover, given the rapid change in the nature of the product— for example, the shift in the ratio of single-section and multi-section MHs from 9:1 to 2:1 over the 10-year period, and the dramatic entrance of the federal government into a direct regulatory role, with the 1976 imposition of HUD's Construction and Safety Standards—one would expect the development of new law and test cases. Such is not the case, however, indicative of the persistence of historic attitudes toward this housing form.

Three topics dominate in the laws and court cases of the decade:

1. Are MHs residences?
2. Are MHs nuisances?
3. What are the rights of MH park owners and residents?

Are MHs Residences?

This issue is raised on narrow legal grounds as well as broader grounds of local policy. The legal grounds result from the initial classification of MHs as personal property, a consequence of their original literal mobility. In most instances the issue has relevance in terms of the tax treatment of the unit; many states, therefore, provide explicit guidance on determining how an MH is converted from personal to real property. In most respects the critical factor is the "affixation" of unit to land in a permanent manner.

On the issue of MHs as residences, most cases reflect an attempt to make a value judgment about what constitutes a "real" residence. The historically nomadic nature of this housing form has served to categorize it as "not a real house," thus effecting the exclusion (de facto, if not de jure) of MHs from residential zones and restricting them to MH park or commercial zones. In reading the cases, one is struck by the awkwardness of the courts' attempts to define a "real" house.

Are MHs Nuisances?

A second broad issue is the impact of MHs on surrounding uses, an issue—even more than the question of the appropriateness of MHs as residences—rooted in the historic nature of this housing form. The cases are characterized more by emotion and are variously confusing, quixotic, and contradictory as sources of public policy guidance. In general, the issue is raised in terms of the proper application of the zoning power to minimize harm caused by one land use to surrounding uses. Historically, the courts have played a conservative role, only slowly changing their attitudes in protecting individual property rights. Because of the unique structural attributes of MHs and the historic use of metal materials for exterior siding, MHs are readily stereotyped and are easy targets for public passions. The nature of the argumentation in the various cases reveals little in the way of increased clarity, from either proponents or opponents. The difficulties associated with determining the impact of various uses on the value of other uses, especially in a projective way, characterizes much of the debate evidenced in these cases more by acrimony than assiduousness.

What Are the Rights of MH Park Owners and Residents?

A subset of the cases deals with the relative rights of MH park owners and residents. Again, given the number of these situations and the unique nature of the relationship of residents (who typically own their units) and park owners (who own the land), it is surprising that the amount of case law on this topic is so sparse. Moreover, when one thinks of the amount of tenant-landlord law created by the social activism of the 1960s and 1970s, the minimal precedent for this housing situation is even more surprising. What tends to confuse things here is that both parties are property owners, leaving little in the way of common law tradition to provide guidance to judicial determinations.

Possible Trends

Two kinds of formalized efforts are now evidence of an attempt to make sense of the legal status of MHs. The first effort, aimed at eliminating barriers to choice, is directed toward *prohibiting exclusion* of this housing form. California, Oregon, Vermont, and Florida, have enacted such legislation within the past few years. The second effort, of an incentive variety, is aimed at *prompting inclusion.* California's definition of MHs as real property is one example, inasmuch as localities will receive a greater tax yield from this housing form. Similarly, San Diego County's "no-frills" MH park ordinance effects a higher return on land than prior zoning restrictions, thus making such investments in the real estate market more attractive.

Notes

1. Material in this chapter is drawn from two reports issued by the Joint Center for Urban Studies, Nutt-Powell et. al., 1980*b*, and Furlong and Nutt-Powell, 1980. Detailed state-by-state information is found in these reports, which are available from the Joint Center.
2. The commission's report, issued in October 1980, reviewed supply and demand, land-use controls, taxation, and financing issues. Its recommendations can be characterized as urging equivalent treatment for MHs in these areas.
3. The legislation has a "hold-harmless" provision, allowing resident owners of MHs purchased before July 1980 to maintain their prior tax status.

Chapter 6

THE FEDERAL GOVERNMENT AND MANUFACTURED HOMES

Public sector attitudes and actions at the local and state levels influence housing markets primarily through the planning for and implementation of acceptable uses of land. Chapter 5 reviewed the various policy and program mechanisms used by states and localities relative to housing markets, including formal policy statement, tax treatment, ownership recording, development controls, financing programs, and technical assistance capabilities.

States enable localities to control the use of land. Consequently, the involvement of these two levels of government in housing markets is direct in terms of what is allowable. The federal government plays a different role, however. At the federal level the concern is whether it is possible to provide various forms of housing; thus most federal programs have a financial focus, either directly (as in provision of mortgage interest subsidies) or indirectly (as in structuring a secondary market). The locational distribution of the resulting housing is not a central concern, whereas the quality of the resulting housing and its sites is because of the need to ensure financial feasibility and fair value.

This chapter reviews various federal policies and programs relating to MHs. The first group of federal agencies—HUD, the VA, Agriculture, and Defense—is directly involved in the provision and financing of housing. The second group—FNMA, GNMA, FHLMC, FHLBB—has an indirect impact on financing through secondary market and finance regulation activities. The third, the FTC, impacts MHs through its consumer protection activities.

Department of Housing and Urban Development

HUD is involved in a variety of financing and subsidy programs, as well as in housing policy and program development.

Financing

HUD has a variety of programs relating to the financial costs of MHs. MH loan insurance is provided under the Title I program. The Section 207 MH park program provides loan insurance for construction or rehabilitation of MH parks. Section 8 provides rental assistance to eligible households for unit and space rental, or for space rental only for occupant-owned units.

Title I MH Loans. Under the Title I program, authorized by the Congress in 1969, HUD insures private lenders against losses for up to 90 percent of the loan amount. Title I loans may be made for purchase of a new or existing MH, a lot for MH use, or the unit and lot in combination; site preparation costs are also eligible for financing. Table 6–1 summarizes the financing terms for loans insured under the Title I program. Because the Title I program is definitionally for units that remain in the personal property category, loans under the program are personal loans secured by conditional sales contracts or chattel mortgages on the MHs. The authorized loan amount, varying according to unit size and whether the land cost is included, ranges from a maximum of $20,000 on a single-section MH without land, to a maximum of nearly $41,000 for a multisection MH on improved land. The maximum terms of loan maturities authorized similarly vary, from 15 to 25 years, according to the nature of the loan. As compared with HUD's Section 203(b) program for site-built single-family dwellings, Title I loans have lower loan maximums, shorter terms of loan maturity, and higher interest rates. In addition to typical applicant financial qualifying standards, HUD has unit and location requirements. The insured unit must meet the HUD Code. If it is not a new unit, it must have been formerly financed with a HUD-insured loan. HUD has site requirements for MH park and borrower-owned locations, including infrastructure, local code, and wind-stabilization system considerations.

Table 6–2 summarizes the amount of loan activity under the Title I program through 1980. The program has shown a steady annual increase in the proportion of units shipped and financed.

Table 6–1   Financing Terms for the Title I MH Loan Program

Type of Loan	Amount of Loan	
	Single-Section	Multisection
MH Loans		
Maximum loan amount	$20,000	$30,000
Maximum term	15 years	23 years
Minimum down payment	5% of 1st $3,000 plus 10% of balance	
MH and Unimproved Lot		
Maximum loan amount	$26,675	$36,675
Maximum term	20 years	25 years
Minimum down payment	5% of 1st $10,000 plus 10% of balance	
MH and Improved Lot		
Maximum loan amount	$30,550	$40,550
Maximum term	20 years	25 years
Minimum down payment	5% of 1st $10,000 plus 10% of balance	
Lot-Only Loans	*Undeveloped*	*Developed*
Maximum loan amount	$6,950	$10,425
Maximum term	15 years	15 years
Minimum down payment	10%	10%
Maximum financing rate (all loans)	18% simple	18% simple
	(17.5% on unit and lot program)	

Note: Table reflects the maximum loan amounts and maximum terms as authorized by the Congress in the Housing and Community Development Act of 1980.

Table 6–2   Title I MH Loan Program, 1970–1980

Calendar Year	Number of Loans	Percent of Total Units Shipped	Amount of Loans ($000)	Average Loan
1970	758	0.2%	$ 6,075	$ 8,014
1971	5,093	1.0	37,077	7,280
1972	6,650	1.2	55,612	8,363
1973	9,239	1.6	85,951	9,303
1974	5,073	1.5	50,503	9,955
1975	7,847	3.7	78,140	9,958
1976	11,580	4.7	129,015	11,141
1977	15,669	5.9	192,306	12,273
1978	22,375	8.1	307,805	13,757
1979	27,774	10.1	414,252	14,915
1980	21,609	9.8	340,820	15,772
Totals	133,667	3.5%	$1,697,556	$12,670

SOURCE: HUD, 1981.

In the last two years Title I loans accounted for about 10 percent of units shipped; the average loan amount in 1980 was $15,772.

Virtually all loans are for MHs only, and nearly all are for new units (HUD, 1981, p. 19). The provision for combination loans on both land and unit, authorized by the Congress in 1974, was implemented in 1977. However, a variety of factors combined to functionally exclude its use. Authorized loan terms and amounts were too low, especially because regulations had no provisions for the lender to charge a loan origination fee. Such loans were not part of the GNMA MH secondary market program. Moreover, the legal issues of land-unit relationship, and the confusions associated with security instruments for the two different forms of legal property, served as barriers to lender interest. Congressional changes to the Title I authorization in 1979 and 1980 addressed these difficulties. Loan maximums were increased, with the amount undifferentiated between land and unit. HUD revised the program regulation to provide a 1 percent loan origination fee. The new regulations were effective in late 1980, with indications of interest and probable increased use.

Section 207 MH Park Program. The Congress authorized the Section 207 MH park loan insurance program in its 1955 amendments to the Housing Act. The program assists in the financing of new MH rental parks and the acquisition and substantial rehabilitation of existing parks. Current statutory authorization provides a mortgage maximum of $8,000 per MH space or 90 percent of HUD's estimate of postconstruction value, whichever is less. Rehabilitation projects not involving land financing are eligible for 100 percent financing of rehab costs. As in many other construction programs, the Congress has authorized higher loan limits at the discretion of the HUD Secretary. The maximum mortgage term is forty years or three fourths of the remaining useful life, whichever is less. The maximum interest rates are generally at the same rate as HUD's other multifamily mortgage insurance programs. HUD also controls maximum rental fee, with provisions for periodic increases due to increased operating and maintenance costs. There are minimum design standards, as well as requirements that the park must adequately provide for families with children.

During the first 15 years of the program, total loan activity was less than $7.5 million. Program activity, summarized in Table 6–3,

Table 6–3   Section 207 MH Park Loan Program, 1970–1979

Calendar Year	Type of Project	Number of Loans	Number of Spaces	Loan Amount ($000)	Average Loan per Space
1970	New	88	15,238	$ 43,596	$2,861
	Rehab	3	366	1,222	3,339
1971	New	154	26,489	82,505	3,115
	Rehab	3	561	1,444	2,574
1972	New	64	10,895	32,894	3,019
1973	New	18	2,807	8,865	3,158
1974	New	8	1,265	3,972	3,140
1975	New	4	862	2,765	3,208
1976	New	6	895	2,576	2,878
	Rehab	1	218	450	2,064
1977	New	2	171	727	4,251
1978	New	2	354	1,639	4,630
	Rehab	1	284	1,250	4,401
1979	New	1	131	453	3,458
	Rehab	1	217	931	4,290
1980	New	0	0	0	0
	Rehab	0	0	0	0
Totals		356	60,753	$185,289	$3,050

SOURCE: HUD, 1981.

occurred almost entirely in the early 1970s. Of the 356 loans made from 1970 to 1980, 312 were made between 1970 and 1972. Total loan activity was approximately $185 million, with an average loan per space of $3,050.

The 1979 amendments to the Housing Act upped the loan limit from $3,900 to $8,000 per space, in the hope that the program would again become a viable tool in providing locations for MH units. No loans were made in 1980, yet program activity did increase, with several proposals beginning the review and approval process. By May 1981, seven projects were being processed, totaling 1,492 unit spaces. The projected loan amounts totaled nearly $6.7 million, for a per space cost of $4,487. Two projects were under construction, totaling 206 unit spaces, with loan amounts totaling $486,000.

Section 8 Program.   HUD's Section 8 program provides rental assistance to low-income families. The Section 8 program is administratively divided according to whether the housing unit is new to the market or part of the existing housing stock. For some years MHs, whether in parks or on individual sites, have been eligible under the Section 8-existing program if part of the rental housing stock. As with other existing rental units, the MH unit must meet HUD's housing quality standards to qualify for the program. HUD applies the same basic standards to MHs as to other types of units, with the addition of certain requirements regarding wind stabilization systems.

In 1978 the Congress authorized the extension of the Section 8-existing program to include rental assistance for MH owners in parks. This authorization was implemented in mid-1979 with regulations governing the calculation of assistance payment relative to space rental. The initial calculation also provides for assistance in unit setup and utility hookup charges. The regulations also amended the housing quality standards to require that any MH unit receiving Section 8-existing assistance have at least one smoke detector. The House version of the 1981 Housing Bill contained a provision that would allow developers of new or substantially rehabilitated MH parks to reserve Section 8 assistance for MH owners who will live in the park. Contracts for assistance under the Section 8-new program would last from 20 to 30 years, the same term that applies to other types of newly constructed or substantially rehabilitated housing that qualifies for the Section 8-new program.[1]

Policy and Program Development

HUD's basic mission is the adequate provision of housing for the American people. Its direct programs use various financial mechanisms to ease market activities, including direct involvement in areas the market is unable to handle independently. In addition to these primarily finance-related activities, HUD undertakes policy and program initiatives pertinent to defining and meeting housing needs. This section considers the impact of several such initiatives on MHs.

The housing cost crisis of the 1970s was severe, as the price of new housing escalated dramatically. The cost comparison of MHs and site-built single-family dwellings would suggest that MHs are a compelling alternative. However, questions of construction quality and life safety have precluded serious consideration of MH integration, on a basis of functional equivalency, into federal housing programs. Indeed it was not until 1980 and 1981 that HUD began to consider MHs on other than a unit-quality problem basis.

The July 1973 hearings leading to the 1974 MH Construction and Safety Standards Act focused on the need to ensure that MHs were in fact decent and safe housing. Witnesses pointed to life safety issues and to the resultant improvements in MH quality from the implementation of state programs. In its testimony, the MH industry supported the proposed legislation. In the act Congress declared as purposes the reduction of personal injuries and deaths and of insurance costs and property damage resulting from MHs.

Given this record of congressional intent, it is not surprising that HUD devoted its energies to code-related questions. HUD's Construction and Safety Standards, and the research related to the adequacy of these standards, are discussed at length in Chapter 3. During the period FY75 through FY80 approximately $4.8 million was expended on research and testing related to the HUD Code (HUD, 1980, p. V-3).

The research did serve its intended purpose of providing clear evidence of state-of-the-art construction quality in MHs. That evidence has allowed policy and program developers to conclude that MHs meet the minimum standards associated with the housing policy phrase "decent, safe and sanitary."[2] Whereas in 1974 Congress determined, in effect, that MHs were not good enough, policymakers in 1980 could view MHs as acceptable and could begin looking to how they might usefully fit into housing strategies with other types of "good enough" units.[3]

One such consideration is the use of MHs as part of HUD's Section 203(b) single-family loan program (HUD, 1981). MHs had been definitionally excluded from this program because they are built to the HUD Code rather than HUD's Minimum Property Standards (MPS) for one- and two-family dwellings.

In August 1980 the Assistant Secretary for Housing issued a notice permitting 203(b) financing for permanently sited, *existing* multisection MHs classified as real estate. By comparison, a January 1981 HUD notice required that *new* multisection MHs be built in accordance with HUD's MPS, or a Structural Engineering

Bulletin (SEB) issued by HUD, or applicable state codes governing manufactured housing. (Permanent siting and real property status were also required.) This structural requirement simply converted the unit from a HUD MH Code review to a HUD or state manufactured housing standard (Danner, 1981). This apparent contradiction in policy was not well received by the MH industry, which contended that a structure acceptable the day after siting should be acceptable the day before siting as well. In partial response to these issues, Housing Deputy Assistant Secretary Abrams convened a group of building trade association representatives (including representatives from the MH industry), code officials, and financers to consider issues related to achieving a single applicable code standard.[4]

Though the comparable quality issues remain a sticking point on particular programs, the general premise of considering MHs in relation to HUD's various funding programs is beginning to receive attention. In January 1981 HUD issued a Report to the Congress on policy and program recommendations to encourage land ownership in MH communities (HUD, 1981). Written by the Office of Policy and Budget in the Office of Housing, the report made both administrative and legislative recommendations, with particular reference to condominium and cooperative arrangements for MH parks. A variety of changes were proposed to render the HUD Section 234 program (condominium) useful in MH settings. Similarly, necessary changes were identified in the Title I and Section 207 programs to provide for cooperative ownership in MH parks.

Indicative of the changing disposition within HUD toward MHs is the different treatment given this housing form by two of its "task force" groups, each with relatively similar composition and mandate. In 1977 HUD convened a task force on housing costs. Its 46 members were selected to represent interests of the private housing sector, consumers, academia, and all levels of government. The report of the task force, issued in May 1978, looks broadly at housing cost problems—particularly land supply and development, building and technology, financing, money markets, and marketing. A series of recommendations were made relative to a nationwide housing cost reduction program. Interestingly, the report made no mention of MHs—indeed, this housing form seems not to have been considered. For example, in

discussing the question of code requirements, the task force explicitly did not recommend federal preemption of state and local
building codes despite the existence of such a code for MHs
(HUD, 1978, p. 37). A close reading leads one to conclude that
the task force was unaware of the preemptive HUD MH Code.

The Council on Development Choices for the '80s, formed in
1980 under HUD sponsorship, was a 37-member bipartisan group
representing all the major participants in the development process:
elected state and local officials developers and business people,
design professionals, and experts from the financial community.
Its mandate was to consider and make recommendations on
emerging development issues in the context of social, economic,
and environmental change. In particular it focused on six areas:
energy consumption, economic development, housing affordability, social and economic mobility, profitability in development,
and provision of public facilities and services. In contrast with
the task force on housing costs, which remained mute on MHs,
the council's final report spoke directly on the MH question, as
well as making recommendations relative to the related set of
institutional barriers influencing various affordability solutions,
including MHs. The council encouraged the use of performance
standards in housing and building codes as a means of fostering
innovation. It asserted that automatic regulatory distinctions between MHs and other housing forms were unjustified and urged
localities to remove arbitrary zoning and subdivision restrictions.
A change in MH tax status was encouraged for both tax base and
housing access reasons. The need for improvement in financing
programs at both state and federal levels was identified (DC '80s,
1981). Although these recommendations were but part of a much
larger report, the inclusion of the issue of MHs in such a major
policy effort is indicative of the shift in orientation of HUD policymakers toward this housing form.

One programmatic indication of this shift is HUD's participation in an MH park rehabilitation effort in Fairfax County,
Virginia. The county is purchasing a 500-unit MH park, for which
65 substandard units will be acquired and cleared. Through a
rehab loan program, owners of 345 other units will be assisted in
making major and minor repairs. Adjacent land will be added to
the park to serve as a relocation resource; recreational and other
amenities will be developed. When completed the park will have

400 units, with a reduction in density from 12.8 to 8.2 units per acre. The project is managed by the Fairfax County Department of Housing and Community Development, using Community Development Block Grant, HUD Innovative Grant, and Section 207 funds. Total project cost is estimated at $9.1 million (HUD, 1981, p. 28).

Veterans Administration

The Veterans Administration MH program, authorized in the Veterans Housing Act of 1970, guarantees loans made by private lenders on new or existing MHs with or without land. It also provides for land-only purchase when the MH unit is already owned. Both veterans and active duty service personnel are eligible for the program.

As compared with the HUD program, the VA has no maximum loan amounts set by legislation. For new MHs there is no VA loan maximum. The maximum loan amount for an existing unit, or a lot purchase, is determined by appraisal. For either a new or existing unit, the VA guarantees the lender against losses up to a maximum of 50 percent of the loan or $20,000, whichever is lower. Furthermore, the VA does not require a down payment. Table 6–4 compares loan conditions for VA and FHA Title I MH loan programs for new MHs. With roughly comparable terms, the VA has a shorter maximum term for multisection MH loans. Its lower interest rates result from the VA program providing a loan guarantee rather than loan insurance; rates therefore do not include a mortgage insurance premium. Lot loans have a maximum term of 12 years, with the rate generally the same as for HUD's Section 203(b) program.

New MHs in the VA program must be built to the HUD Code. Existing units, which have the same general terms and conditions for loan guarantees, are subject to VA determination of remaining physical life. Unit locations, whether in a park or on an owned site, must be VA-approved. Multisection MHs in an MH park must have a three-year lease; MHs in subdivisions or planned unit developments must meet VA single-family dwelling site design requirements.

Table 6–4 Comparison of VA and FHA (Title I) Financing of New MHs

	VA	FHA
MH Only		
Single-section		
Loan maximum	None	$20,000
Term maximum	15 years	15 years
Multisection		
Loan maximum	None	$30,000
Term maximum	20 years	23 years
Maximum guaranty	$20,000 or 50% of loan, whichever is less	See above
Rate ceiling*	17.5%	18%
Down payment	None required	5% of first $3,000, plus 10% of amount over $3,000
MH Plus Improved Land		
Single-section		
Loan maximum	None	$30,550
Term maximum	15 years	20 years
Multisection		
Loan maximum	None	$40,550
Term maximum	20 years	25 years
Maximum guaranty	$20,000 or 50% of loan, whichever is less	See above
Rate ceiling*	17%	17.5%
Down payment	None required	5% of first $3,000, plus 10% of amount over $3,000

SOURCE: VA, HUD.

* Ceiling as of June 1981.

The VA program began operations in 1971. Table 6–5, summarizing program activity, shows that through April 30, 1981, 82 percent of the 47,484 loans guaranteed were for single-section MHs. Moreover, almost all loans were for new units. Slightly more than three fourths of all units were placed in MH parks. Although the VA's unit and lot program has been in effect since 1974, only 3.9 percent of loans have involved guarantees on lot as well as unit.

Table 6–5   Summary of VA MH Loan Operations Through April 30, 1981

	Number of Loans	Amount of Loans	Average Amount of Loans
Total MH loans	47,484	$667,068,773	$14,048
Paid in full	5,716	54,978,557	9,618
MH Loan Classification			
MH only-rented space	36,625	483,779,625	13,209
MH only-own lot	8,986	158,249,328	17,646
MH and site preparation	159	2,332,530	14,670
MH undeveloped lot, and site preparation	223	2,695,178	12,086
MH and developed site	1,491	19,694,619	13,209
MH lot only	5	34,785	6,957
MH Type of Structure			
Single-section	38,955	478,857,444	12,293
Multisection	8,529	188,211,329	22,067
New MH	46,010	640,043,926	13,910
Existing MH	1,474	27,024,847	18,334

SOURCE: VA, unpublished data, 1981.

Note: "MH lot only" not included in "total MH loans."

Table 6–6   VA MH Loan Program, 1971–1980

Calendar Year	Number of Loans	Percent of Total Units Shipped	Amount of Loans (1000's)	Average Loan
1971	2,080	0.4	$ 17,424	$ 8,377
1972	5,460	0.9	47,452	8,691
1973	6,014	1.1	54,036	8,985
1974	3,381	1.0	30,777	9,103
1975	1,679	0.8	18,163	10,818
1976	1,566	0.6	19,437	12,412
1977	3,459	1.3	46,257	13,373
1978	4,104	1.5	57,169	13,930
1979	8,551	3.1	156,166	18,263
1980	7,937	3.6	156,423	19,708
Totals	44,231	1.3	$603,304	$13,640

SOURCE: VA, unpublished data, 1981.

Table 6–6 presents a summary of the VA program by year, through 1980. The proportion of MH units purchased with VA financing has increased steadily for the past five years, from only 0.6 percent in 1976, at an average loan amount of $12,412, to 3.6 percent in 1980, with an average loan amount of $19,708. VA loan activity through April 1981 totaled over $667 million, at an average of $14,048. The 1978 changes in enabling legislation, including elimination of statutory maximum loan amounts and increases in maximum terms, made the VA program more attractive. These changes account for the major increases in loan activity in 1979 and 1980.

Department of Agriculture

Although the Farmers Home Administration (FmHA) was authorized to establish an MH loan program in 1974, such a program has not yet been created. FmHA did place a notice of intent to begin developing an MH program and asked for comments in the *Federal Register* in October 1980. FmHA officials have indicated concerns about the real versus personal property status and have indicated a disposition to require permanent foundations. They are uncertain, however, about the possible clientele for such a program. Similarly, they are unresolved about how to meet the statutory requirement to prescribe minimum property standards to assure MH livability and durability and the suitability of the proposed site. There is some indication that the HUD standards will be sufficient.[5] Following budget hearings in spring of 1981, FmHA officials agreed to work with staff of the Senate Housing Subcommittee toward expeditious implementation of an MH loan program.

Department of Defense

Although the VA provides loan guarantees for MH purchase to active service personnel, the Department of Defense (DOD) has only recently considered the use of MHs in its housing programs. DOD interest in MHs has been prompted by the Congress and by its own perceived need to provide more low-cost housing. This latter need will be substantial if a policy to expand eligibility for military base housing, now under consideration, is implemented.[6]

DOD is in the early stages of one assessment of MHs and may undertake a second during 1982. The first project is at Fallon Naval Air Station in Nevada, where 70 two-bedroom multisection MH units are being located at the base. In devising specifications for the MH units, HUD MH code standards were upgraded in the areas of fire safety (gypsum wallboard in lieu of plywood paneling wall finish), energy conservation (insulation to meet Zone 3—Alaska—standard), and operations and maintenance items (garbage disposals from 1/3 HP to 1/2 HP, for example). Upgrading in this last area reflected DOD field experience for rental quarters on military bases, which average a tenant turnover at least once every two years. The FOB factory cost per unit was $18,241, approximately $2,000 of which was attributable to DOD's requested specification changes.

Operating, maintenance, and structural durability character-istics of these units will be compared with 106 existing site-built units constructed in 1962. The units will be monitored for a five-year period, with particular attention to trouble calls, high main-tenance items (carpet, appliances, hardware, and so on), exterior finish, and energy consumption. At the completion of the five-year comparison, at least 20 percent of the units will be inspected to determine overall condition and rehabilitation requirements. Pre- and postoccupancy resident attitudes will also be measured.[7]

The second assessment proposed for 1982 by the House Sub-committee on Military Installations and Facilities, would compare 200 MH and 254 site-built units at the Army's National Training Center, Fort Irwin, near Barstow, California. (The proposal was still under congressional review in the fall of 1981.) As compared with the Fallon project, the Fort Irwin demonstration will com-pare units built at the same time, to approximately the same specifications. As at Fallon, the units are two bedrooms and will have many of the same specifications changes as at Fallon. Again, longitudinal studies of operating and maintenance requirements, life-cycle costs, and behavioral impact will be conducted.

Federal National Mortgage Association

The Federal National Mortgage Association (FNMA) is a pri-vately owned and managed corporation whose main purpose is to supplement the secondary market for residential mortgages. Its purchase activities provide additional liquidity to the market and improve the distribution of available investment capital. FNMA became a private corporation in 1968 with its former public functions carried on by the Government National Mortgage Association (GNMA). In its first 10 years of private operation, the FNMA provided financing for both new and existing dwellings housing more than 2.5 million families (FNMA, 1979).

The FNMA has a variety of mortgage purchase programs. Over one half of the dollar amount of the FNMA's mortgage portfolio consists of one- to four-family mortgages insured by the FHA or guaranteed by the VA (FNMA, 1979, p. 21). Additionally, the FNMA purchases government-insured project mortgages, federally subsidized mortgages, conventional one- to four-family mortgages (including special condominium and PUD programs), and participates in construction advances. The FNMA has several urban-oriented programs, including one begun in 1979 that provides long-term financing in urban areas for the rehabilitation of one- to four-family homes.

The FNMA's only MH specific program is the purchase of GNMA-guaranteed certificates backed by pools of FHA/VA MH loans. The minimum commitment amount is $500,000 with no maximum. The yield is set for the total commitment amount and is equal to the weighted average yield of the FHA/VA Free Market Auction in effect (FNMA, 1981a, p. 80–H).

The FNMA has provided a prequalification program for manufactured housing built to state as well as the HUD Code. To facilitate the marketing and financing of these homes, the FNMA will review and analyze plans and specifications for units at the request of a manufacturer. A letter outlining all conditions of FNMA's approval will then be provided to the manufacturer for use with developers and lenders. Approval is generally unconditional as to the location of the units, yet the program applies only to units designed for placement on a conventional foundation. In all cases, units must be attached to a permanent foundation and must qualify as real property under local law (FNMA, 1981a, p. 80–R). In these situations, the FNMA's existing mortgage purchase programs are used. Among the 29 manufacturers that had currently qualified units as of April 1, 1981, the FNMA's listing of accepted unit types identified 631 different models (FNMA, 1981b, pp. 1–19). The August 1981 new policy (reviewed later in this chapter) eliminated further need for this program.

In June 1976 the FNMA initiated a study of MH personal property purchase paper; in June 1977 an interim report was completed, but not made public. The effort constituted a major assessment by FNMA personnel of the feasibility of FNMA's entry into this housing market area. The report reviewed the profitability of MH lending, the legal implications and problems implicit in the financing of loans secured by personal property, and the potential impact of FNMA participation on the MH industry.

The sticking point for the FNMA's entry into this secondary market activity is the personal property classification of MHs. An opinion from the FNMA's general counsel for the study concluded that the FNMA was not authorized to purchase conventional loans secured by chattel mortgages on MH units. The differences among states in codes governing consumer credit provided additional barriers to positive consideration.

In 1980 the Congress authorized FNMA creation of an MH-Personal Property secondary market program. Although FNMA staff devised a program in response to the congressional mandate, the transition in administrations (which included shifts in FNMA top management) precluded the program's movement beyond preliminary internal review.

In early 1981 FNMA also suspended its MH-Real Property activities pending an interpretation from the Federal Home Loan Bank Board (FHLBB) on which MH forms were subject to usury preemption regulations. This action illustrates the particular difficulty with the MH having two possible legal statuses, with the distinction rather fuzzy. Usury regulations would cover MHs financed under commercial credit codes and would have the effect of prohibiting various negotiable interest rates. Since this mechanism is increasingly used in shelter loans (including MH real estate), the exclusion of some or all MHS would have a serious impact on the MH secondary market.

In late July, the FHLBB replied to the FNMA request by indicating that, for its purposes, an MH was real property under the following circumstances:

> *Regardless of state law, however, it is our opinion that the mobile home/lot combinations which FNMA intends to finance should be treated as residential real property for purposes of the federal usury preemption. When all the facts and circumstances are considered, it appears that real property is the only logical*

category for this security. First, when the wheels and axles are removed and the unit is permanently affixed to a foundation, these homes are no more mobile than traditional housing. Second, like a conventional real property transaction, both the mobile home and lot are conveyed together and covered by a standard real estate title insurance policy. Third, the sale is financed in the manner customarily used in real estate transactions, using an interest bearing note rather than a precomputed interest contract. Accordingly, there is no problem with Rule of 78s rebates. Fourth, although a personal lien may be recorded as a precaution, foreclosure must conform to real estate statutes. (In the instant case, these third and fourth factors will be present because the FNMA/ FHLMC uniform mortgage is used.) In our view, whenever these four factors are present, a mobile home and lot combination may be considered residential real property for purposes of the federal usury preemption and a loan secured by such a combination need not incorporate the consumer protections required by Section 590.4 of our regulations.[8]

In early August the FNMA announced that it would apply its general SFD borrower credit and property guidelines in secondary market mortgage purchases of MHs meeting these standards.[9]

Government National Mortgage Association

The Government National Mortgage Association (GNMA) is a wholly owned government corporation within HUD. GNMA was created in 1968 when the original publicly owned FNMA was split into two corporations, one public (GNMA) and one private (FNMA). GNMA's secondary market activities are funded mainly from borrowing from the U.S. Treasury. Its primary objective is to supply mortgage credit in support of government housing objectives. Many of the GNMA's day-to-day activities are performed under contract by FNMA.

A major GNMA program is its issuance of mortgage-backed securities. The GNMA guarantees the timely payment of principal and interest on securities issued to investors by holders of pools of mortgages, which constitute the assets backing the securities. These mortgage pools involve mortgages insured or guaranteed by the FHA, VA, and/or FmMA. The GNMA guaranty is backed by the full faith and credit of the United States. HUD MH Title I (including unit and lot loans, given recent changes in regulations)

Table 6–7   GNMA MH-Mortgage-Backed Securities Activity, 1972
Through May 1981

Year	Amount ($ in millions)
1972	4.7
1973	42.6
1974	36.4
1975	55.8
1976	90.9
1977	161.8
1978	257.0
1979	408.7
1980	483.9
1981 (through May)	165.3
Total	1,707.1

Source: GNMA, unpublished data, 1981.

Note: Total all GNMA activities: $120,000 (approximate); MH activities as percent of total: 1.4.

and VA MH loans are among the programs included in the GNMA Mortgage-Backed Securities (MBS) program.

Table 6–7 summarizes GNMA activity in MH-mortgage-backed securities since this program became active in 1972. Through May 1981 GNMA had packaged approximately $1.7 billion in MH-mortgage-backed securities, representing about 1.4 percent of total GNMA activities. Table 6–8 summarizes the number of

Table 6–8   MH Units Involved in GNMA Mortgage-Backed Securities
Pool, FY 1972 Through May 1981

FY	FHA	VA	Total
1972	257	—	257
1973	4,279	—	4,279
1974	3,025	—	3,025
1975	3,931	—	3,931
1976	7,911	—	7,911
1977	10,179	385	10,564
1978	14,136	2,671	16,807
1979	20,226	4,132	24,358
1980	20,942	7,215	28,157
1981 (through May)	12,867	4,843	17,710
Total	97,753	19,246	116,999

Source: GNMA, unpublished data, 1981.

MH units covered in the MH MSB pools. Through May 1981, 116,999 units were involved, of which about 84 percent were FHA. GNMA's MH program accounts for nearly three fourths of FHA Title I loans and two fifths of VA MH loans.

In 1980 the GNMA issued changes to the Mortgage-Backed Securities Guide with particular reference to MH loan pools. Various issues relating to the combination unit and land loans were resolved, including cross-collateralization of separate unit and lot instruments. The changes also allowed for a minimum of only $350,000 in pools containing at least one unit and lot loan, compared with $500,000 for pools of unit-only loans (GNMA, 1980).

Federal Home Loan Bank Board

The Federal Home Loan Bank Board (FHLBB), as well as regulating the savings and loan industry, provides a source of secondary housing credit. Part of the Bank Board's regulatory activities cover permissible S&L activities in relation to MH lending. (Chapter 3 reviewed trends in amounts and sources of financing.)

Little attention was given to MH lending by the Bank Board through much of the 1970s. Most public comments related either to technical modifications in regulations (for example, stipulations for flood insurance prior to lending if the MH was in a flood zone). In 1973 the Bank Board announced an increase in maximum maturities on new MHs and differentiated loan treatment by unit size. Loan maturities on existing units were also increased, with the permissible limits a function of the unit age.

However in 1977, Grady Perry Jr, then a member of the Bank Board, noted the possibilities for MHs in an address to the U.S. League of Savings Associations. In his address Perry identified nine initiatives for the board and the S&L industry. Of the eighth, low-cost housing, Perry said:

The least expensive housing in the country today is manufactured. Mobile homes account for almost all the homes purchased under $15,000. And yet these low-income home buyers must pay the highest interest rates in the market—consumer rates in the neighborhood of, say, 12 to 13 percent. We all know that there have been problems with mobile homes, particularly with trying to finance a non-durable property on a long-term mortgage basis. On the other hand, we all know mobile homes are changing. The line

between the traditional mobile home and high-quality manufac-
tured homes has blurred. HUD's new safety standards are upgrad-
ing the whole industry. It may well be that the time is here to
consider making longer term mortgage financing available on
manufactured and mobile homes purchased with a lot within the
constraints raised by the expected life of the property. By doing
so, we could bring some of the advantages of home ownership to
people with lower incomes. (Perry, 1977, pp. 4–5)

Perry's remarks apparently prompted some internal considerations. Joseph Horton, a visiting economist in the Bank Board's Office of Economic Research, published a review of MH lending in the *FHLBB Journal*, March 1979 issue (Horton, 1979). The article, which summarized internal research and discussions, reached several conclusions about MH lending and possible Bank Board changes. Horton found that while MH loans in aggregate were somewhat more risky than most other loans made by S&Ls, this conclusion was not universally true. Moreover, Horton found that then current regulations did not place the risk exposure of federal associations below that of state S&Ls. The thrust of Horton's conclusions was that the Bank Board could liberalize its MH lending regulations without placing its regulated associations in a position of undue risk.

In fact such a liberalization was announced in the summer of 1979. In issuing its new regulations, the Bank Board noted that MHs had become an attractive housing option. It suggested that the new regulations would enable S&Ls to develop underwriting policies appropriate to the changing nature of the housing and its markets.

The regulations were changed in three areas. First, loans were permitted up to 90 percent of total cost, including related items such as transportation, setup, taxes, and so on, thus effecting the lowering of down payment requirements from 15 percent to 10 percent. Second, terms of maturity were extended to 20 years for both new and existing units, thus constituting an increase from 12- and 15-year maturities. Finally, a S&L was permitted to extend total MH financing to 20 percent of total assets, up from 10 percent. Moreover, participation in the purchase and sale of participation interests in MH paper was liberalized. Retention requirements for sellers of MH paper were reduced from 50 percent to 25 percent. This reduction, combined with the increased lending authority, expanded the potential flow of funds. The

Bank Board did limit S&Ls to purchasing MH paper only from an institution whose accounts or deposits were insured by the FSLIC, FDIC, or the Nation Credit Union Administration, or a service corporation of such an institution.

The July 1981 FHLBB ruling on its definition of MH real property, discussed in connection with the FNMA's activities, is a major statement of policy in the financing community.

The Federal Home Loan Mortgage Corporation (FHLMC) serves a secondary market function for secondary mortgages. As the three members of the FHLBB are the FHLMC's board of directors, its functions are closely related to Bank Board objectives. FHLMC buys mortgages and interests in mortgages secured by homes and multifamily properties. The sellers are principally S&Ls and the mortgages primarily conventional. However, FHLMC has no MH program, despite the liberalization in Bank Board regulations on S&L MH activity.

Federal Trade Commission

The Federal Trade Commission (FTC) has authority to act on various consumer trade issues, notably protection of consumer rights. In September 1972 the FTC authorized a staff investigation of the warranty practices of MH manufacturers. While that investigation was underway, the MH trade association petitioned the FTC for a trade regulation rule on MH warranty service. In its 1980 report on the subsequent rule-making procedure, the FTC staff cited language from this petition as cogently summarizing the need for a rule:

> *The promulgation of a rule ensures that all industry members will be under the same substantive obligations at the same point in time—it avoids the unfairness inherent in singling out a few industry members to bear the adverse publicity and financial burden of defending expensive and time consuming law suits on problems which are of an industry-wide scope. (FTC, 1980, p. 10)*[10]

During the course of the initial investigation, the FTC entered into consent orders with four MH manufacturers regarding procedures to improve warranty service.

In May 1975 the FTC published a notice of proposed rule-making on MH sales and service. That rule-making procedure, including extensive public hearings and period of public comment, was still continuing in the summer of 1981. A final staff report and proposed Trade Regulation Rule was issued in August 1980 and is discussed below. The formal comment period following the issuance of the report was extended from the normal two to six months, at industry request. The comment period closed the end of February 1981. The succeeding steps include a summary of received comments, staff proposals for modification to the proposed rule, recommendations from the FTC's Director of the Bureau of Consumer Protection, commission consideration (including the possibility of a brief period for oral presentations), commission decision, and congressional review.

The rule making dealt primarily with warranty issues, including service, delegation, monitoring, and representations. In the 1980 report, the FTC staff made the following findings and recommendations: Timely and full warranty service was such a sufficiently frequent problem that the staff recommended a rule requiring complete warranty service within 30 days after receiving a request for repairs. (A five-day period was recommended for emergency conditions.) The staff also recommended a required inspection of each new MH after installation at the homesite.

The staff found the manner in which warranty service was delegated to be a significant cause of inadequate warranty service. The delegation of responsibility from the MH manufacturer to the dealer, in whole or in part, was found to be often ambiguous and ill-defined. FTC staff, therefore, recommended a clear definition of terms and conditions of service delegation. Related to the service delegation issue is the monitoring of service activities. As needed improvements in the monitoring process, FTC staff recommended improvements in manufacturer record keeping, as well as a buyer questionnaire as part of the warranty materials.

The FTC found that although transportation and setup were common sources of defects in new MHs, many manufacturers exclude these functions from their warranties. The staff recommended inclusion of these functions in manufacturer warranties. The FTC also made findings relate to specific coverage of warranty and representations of unit size, with recommendations on clarification in each case (FTC, 1980).

The FTC's rule-making procedure on MH sales and service practices spanned a time period during which significant changes were occurring in consumer protection attitudes throughout the country. Initially supporting the effort, the MH industry shifted its position to one of systematic opposition, claiming that the HUD Code requirements were both preemptive of FTC involvement and sufficient for the purposes of consumer protection. The industry also argued that much of what the FTC was proposing as rule, such as unit inspection on setup, was common practice by the end of the decade. Consumer advocate groups, including those with a housing orientation, strongly backed the FTC's efforts. The Congress also intervened in FTC activities more generally, attempting to curtail what some members of Congress felt was excessive zeal by the commission and its staff. The controversy was especially pronounced in 1980, when the Congress refused to extend the FTC's authorizing and appropriating legislation, leaving the FTC technically nonexistent for a period of days. The issue was resolved by legislation providing the Congress with certain override powers on FTC rules. This trend toward deregulation was furthered by supporting policies of the Reagan administration.

Thus by mid-1981, more than nine years after the FTC began its original investigation and six years after it began its formal rule-making process, the outcome was still unclear. The MH industry was continuing its opposition, including a vigorous lobbying campaign with the Congress, while consumer groups continued to support the proposed rule. The FTC staff was preparing its summary of the comments and recommendations for the final proposed language for the rule.

Notes

1. Because the Senate version did not contain this language, its fate depended on the outcome of the reconciliation process, scheduled to occur in June or July of 1981.
2. Two related dynamics also facilitated this conclusion. First, the 1973–1974 recession (and the particularly extreme boom-bust sequence that occurred in the MH industry at that time) forced many of the marginal manufacturers out of business. Second, the 1976 imposition of the HUD Code ensured that *all* units would meet at least the minimum standards. Thus even marginal operators (if any remained) would construct units meeting a publicly determined standard.
3. Although this argument seems somewhat harsh and tortured, in fact publicly established standards can only establish minimums. Moreover,

those standards must connect to the public's health and safety; the causalities must be clear and direct. The debates that continue about the adequacy of MHs from a construction quality and safety perspective revolve around where the minimum is to be set, not whether the current state-of-the-art of MHs meets that minimum. Interestingly, among the HUD research contracts was one that did cost/benefit analyses of the various alternative standards recommendations made by technical contractors. The cost/benefit consultant did not always support the recommendations of technical contractors for "higher" standards.

4. The initial meeting of the group, which included representatives of NCSBCS, CABO, NIBS, NAHM, NAHB, MHI, WMHI, NMHF, MBA, and others was scheduled for July 1, 1981. The agenda included a review of code-related recommendations of major national studies, pertinent existing regulations, the possible phasing out of HUD's Minimum Property Standards in favor of a one- and two-family dwelling code, and a consideration of how the model codes presently handle manufactured housing. (Telephone interview with Earl Flanagan, HUD, June 24, 1981.)

5. Interview with Reed Petersen, FmHA, November 14, 1980.

6. Telephone interview with Patrick Meehan, Director of Housing, DOD, June 18, 1981.

7. Letter to author from Mortimer M. Marshall, Jr., Director, Construction, DOD, June 17, 1981.

8. Letter from Thomas P. Vartanian, General Counsel, FHLBB to Russell B. Clifton, Vice President for Mortgage Programs, FNMA, July 28, 1981.

9. FNMA's guidelines, announced August 6, 1981, included the following:

> *The unit must be permanently attached to a real estate lot, and wheels and axles must be removed;*
> *The land and the home must be sold as a package and financed by a single real estate mortgage;*
> *The mortgage must be covered by a standard title insurance policy;*
> *The mortgage must exclude financing of furniture (except kitchen and laundry appliances, draperies and carpeting) and any kind of insurance; and*
> *The property must be comparable to site-built housing in the local marketplace.*

10. The industry petition was subsequently withdrawn.

Chapter 7

MANUFACTURED HOMES: ISSUES FOR A HOUSING OPPORTUNITY

This book opened with a set of observations about housing problems in the United States and the possible opportunity that manufactured homes hold as part of the solution to those problems. In particular the question was posed as to whether the present relatively limited use of MHs is the result of market imperfections caused by or susceptible to treatment by public and/or private sector actions.

Based on evidence presented in this volume a reasonable answer to that question is yes. The present level of MH use is in many ways a function of public sector attitudes and programs, many of which maintain the historic negative images of this housing form. MHs have been perceived as cheap, flimsy, and unattractive housing intended for undesirable markets. As much of the foregoing discussion has shown, this image does not conform with the reality of contemporary MHs. However historically accurate the negative images, they are no longer a sound basis for public sector attitudes and programs.

A result of these traditional attitudes is that MHs are the bastard child of the housing sector, with no one taking responsibility to nurture their appropriate growth as a housing opportunity. Surprisingly, this general indictment extends to the MH industry as well. Because the industry tends to perpetuate its historic differences from site-built housing (namely mobility and

147

in-plant construction), it frequently acts in a manner essentially inconsistent with what is considered appropriate "housing" behavior. As compared with other segments of the housing sector, the MH industry appears instinctively antagonistic to the public sector. When industry attitudes are combined with public officials' unthinking maintenance of historic images and biases toward MHs, the results are neglect and lost opportunities.

There are, however, signs of change. As noted throughout earlier chapters, sensible and sensitive use of this housing form is evident in housing policies and programs in certain localities, states, and branches of the federal government, and in some areas of the private sector. But, as often as not, that evidence points to the need for further elaboration of the possibilities MHs offer as part of housing policies, programs and activities. The remainder of this chapter is devoted to issues requiring attention if sense is to be made of MHs as a housing opportunity. Areas discussed include unit-specific topics, MH financing, market trends, and legal issues.

Unit-Specific Topics

Two general unit-specific topics derive from the historic image of MHs. The first topic is the intrinsic structural quality (and related occupant safety) of the MH unit. The second topic involves the appearance of MHs and the consequent issue of "fit" in particular locations. Consideration of these topics recurs because of the distinctive rectangular configuration of MHs, one recognizable even in contemporary MHs. It is this structural form that perpetuates the historic images.

The congressional authorization of a preemptive federal code for the construction of a housing type signaled a new era in the history of building codes. Previously, federal involvement in specifying construction standards had been for actuarial purposes, establishing reasonable parameters of financial involvement in housing by the government. By comparison the Congress' 1974 MH Construction and Safety Standards Act provided a construction code for every unit of this type, regardless of the government's financial stake. The rationale for this action was protection of the public health and safety, rather than concern for the government's financial exposure.

The implications of this action need to be taken to their logical conclusion. Two paths of action are possible. The first would be to establish similarly inclusive preemptive construction and safety codes for other housing forms. Both the mood of the country opposing major regulatory initiatives and the absence of an easily recognizable legal basis (such as interstate commerce for MHs) yield this an unlikely approach. A second and somewhat less direct approach would be to undertake rigorous comparative studies of essentially similar housing types built to different codes.[1] Yet a particular limitation of existing MH research is that results are reported in a vacuum. Certain code requirements are unique and necessary to particular construction approaches. However, when comparing relatively equivalent use types (one-floor, single-family detached dwellings, in the case of MHs), there are a substantial number of generic requirements. Direct, objective comparisons of components and aggregate structural quality allow interested participants in the housing sector to reach pertinent decisions about housing types.[2]

An important element in these studies should be information communication in a form meeting the varying needs of participants in the housing sector. Buyers, lenders, code officials, designers, and others each have different uses for comparative structural information. For example, consumers ask questions of the following form that imply a binary answer.

1. Is this good housing?
2. Is this house as good as that house?
3. Is this house as good as that house, in terms of energy, or durability, or safety from storms?

The information required to answer these questions is not the sort provided in a detailed engineering analysis, yet it may be based on it. It may also involve certain cost-constraint tradeoffs not relevant to an engineer's comparative structural analysis. For example, the answer to the question, Is this house as good as that house? may be irrelevant if one house is in the $40,000–$50,000 range, but the other in the $200,000 range. The answer may in fact be yes, but not matter to the consumer who can afford houses only in the lower range.

The second unit-specific topic is the appearance of MHs and the consequent "fit" into particular locations. The rectangular form (which continues in single-section MHs), the traditional metal siding and flat roof, and the absence of permanent foundations have all contributed to a perception of MHs as aesthetically unappealing and deleteriously affecting areas in which they are located. This image is easily reinforced. A look at an early 1960s "pink-and-white trailer" in the middle of a barren plot of land by the side of a highway quickly confirms the prevailing notion. Conversely, contemporary MHs (both single- and multisection) with pitched roofs, attractive exterior siding materials, permanent foundations (or perimeter enclosure systems), and landscaped grounds will tend not to be identified as manufactured homes.

The question of appearance and "fit" is especially difficult, for it entails a determination of the extent of legitimate public sector intervention into matters of taste. Development controls are based on public police powers, with the controls instituted to safeguard the public's health and safety. Controls pertaining to appearance, however, have tended to be limited to special districts, such as areas of special historic significance. Controls governing "fit" are somewhat broader and include such aspects as unit siting, height, and lot coverage. Recent controls also govern the right of solar access. With the change from literal mobility to functional permanence, the premise that MHs are categorically different (and presumptively nonconforming) types of single-family residence is less readily sustained. Indeed that was the thrust of the 1981 Michigan Supreme Court ruling in *Robinson Township* v. *Knoll*.

The reaction, as in the California law, is to provide for design review to establish "fit." This approach leaves the burden of proof on the MH owner (either developer or would-be occupant). Unless equally applied to all SFDs in a proposed area, such an approach could leave local jurisdictions open to claims of unequal treatment before the law. Perhaps as important is that this sort of regulatory approach provides no guidance or assistance to jurisdictions for sensible and sensitive integration of MHs (or any other form of SFD, for that matter) into existing or new residential areas. Indeed, at base, it may well be asked if aesthetic "fit" at this level is a legitimate application of zoning powers.

Clearly, the practices of the MH industry in terms of unit siting have left much to be desired. While in some cases economic exigencies may necessitate minimal initial site improvements, there is no reason for the continued absence of a tradition of unit and lot improvement. If there is an explanation for lack of attention to site-improvement matters, it is in the separation of construction, sales, and occupancy activities in the MH industry. As compared with other forms of housing development, none of the parties responsible for MH construction, sales, or occupancy has a direct responsibility for (and therefore long-term business stake in) site appearance.[3] With few exceptions the MH purchaser does not have the requisite knowledge and/or funds to make the sorts of site improvements that enhance the unit's appearance.

With the business viability of manufacturers, dealers, and transporters not directly affected by unit appearance on site, little has been done to systematically improve this aspect of MHs in housing markets. Moreover, jurisdictions have tended to deal with the problem by excluding its possibility. Given current housing problems, that is a luxury few can continue to afford. Thus a real need for jurisdictions is to acquire the capability to guide sound siting practices and location integration of MHs.

In the absence of private sector initiatives to provide the necessary technical assistance, responsibility to prompt this activity falls to the public sector. Given how diffuse the problem is, this responsibility is best assumed at the federal level, at least in terms of generic materials, such as guides to sensible siting, approaches to effective use of MHs in local housing strategies, and model planning and statutory approaches. State agencies with interests in housing and community development can prepare technical assistance materials with greater location specificity and develop special levels of expertise of regular staff.

Financing

Although MHs have evolved to be functionally permanent residences (regardless of technical affixation), their treatment for financing purposes continues to be complicated by the personal property legal definition. To begin with all MHs are legally personal property. Further, many existing MHs, and most probably a large yet decreasing proportion of new MHs, will not be "affixed" to their sites and will thus remain legally in the personal property category. "Affixed" MHs do become real property although the standards of "affixation" are not uniform among states. Thus a real and continuing need is to devise approaches to MH financing that recognize the unique relationship between land and unit, as well as the functional permanence of the units, whatever the land-unit relationship. Work yielding more appropriate financing practices is necessary in five areas: (1) housing value, (2) ownership recording, (3) mortgage instruments, (4) mortgage terms, and (5) capital availability.

Housing Value

Structural durability is but one factor in determining the value of a house. The comparative durability analyses discussed earlier would shed some light on the market value of MHs (and other housing forms), but only insofar as that market value is determined by the structure per se. In fact the conventional wisdom in determination of real estate value ranks location as the primary factor. The historic limitation of MH locations to a relatively few (and implicitly less desirable) zones, therefore, has skewed the value base. The limitations on locations (primarily to MH parks) and the presumption of mobility (hence structural degradation) combined to support a value premise of depreciation. The present reality is that there are fewer limitations on location and, practically speaking no mobility other than from plant to home site. Thus the traditional bases for a presumption of depreciation are no longer valid.

Appraisal practices have not kept up with the changing role and status of MHs in housing markets. The Foremost study, discussed in Chapter 4, is but a first step toward understanding what factors influence the market value of MHs, and the extent of appreciation (or depreciation) under various conditions. The need to accurately determine value is important for private market transactions. It is even more important in the determination of assessed valuation for public tax roles. California's recent statute subjecting MHs to real property taxation, regardless of affixation, provides evidence of this very need. But the determination of value for public tax purposes is not an easy matter, especially in cases in which the unit and land are owned by different parties. Although there is functional permanence, typically there is not legal permanence. Thus it is not clear how to treat location, site improvements, and similar factors in determining assessed valuation.

Ownership Recording

The present approach to public recording and transfer of MH ownership is at best confused, a consequence of the mobility heritage of this housing form. The recording of ownership of residences serves a function for the owner, lenders, and the public sector. For owners it provides a description of the property owned and of its status relative to use as security for a loan. For lenders it provides a mechanism to secure financial risk. For the public sector it provides a means of identifying the parties legally responsible for the property.

As described in Chapter 5, in most states the form of ownership recording is related to practices for automobiles, with a title recorded with the state's department of motor vehicles. Owners offer as evidence of ownership a bill of sale, which may be accompanied by a certificate of origin.[4] (The probability of an owner having a copy of the certificate of origin decreases after the initial sale.) In states not requiring titling, the unit often will not be titled unless it is financed since the lender requires titling as a means of establishing lien. An alternate means of establishing lien is the filing of a UCC form with a jurisdictional clerk. But if the unit is not financed (and many are purchased with cash), it is unlikely that a continuous, confirmable record of ownership will exist.

Most discussions of improvements in MH ownership recording suggest practices similar to those for other forms of residence. (MHs affixed to real property do become part of the deed, as improvements to the land.) The supporting arguments generally are premised on consumers,' lenders,' and public officials' understanding deed-related recording of ownership. The difficulty in adopting a total real property approach is that in fact some MHs do move after initial location. The recording method, therefore, must allow for this possibility.

This contingency suggests the invention of a new recording instrument, much as it was necessary to invent a method to record condominium ownership. At least three variations are possible:

1. A variation of UCC recording: An ownership instrument would be filed with a municipal clerk.
2. A variation of condo recording: An ownership instrument (unit deed) would be filed with the recorder of deeds with some relationship to the real property (master) deed.

3. A variation of DMV recording: An ownership instrument would be filed with a state agency.

The UCC procedure is similar to that currently employed for commercial code lien recording. The recorder of deeds procedure most closely fits current practice for real property and is similar to a procedure adopted a few years ago in British Columbia. The DMV variation is currently employed in California, with titles issued by the Department of Housing and Community Development.

Because each option entails filing with a public entity, provision can be made to record liens and maintain clear records for public liabilities, including property taxes. Making issuance of transportation permits contingent on evidence that all liens and tax obligations are satisfied would provide the essential guarantees desired by each of the three primarily interested parties.

Mortgage Instruments

As with ownership recording, the issue of appropriate mortgage instruments is complicated because MHs can be moved. Even though size, use, cost, and practical immobility of contemporary MHs would suggest the use of normal shelter loan mechanisms, the unique characteristics of MHs (including the tradition of different land-unit ownership) necessitates the invention of mortgage instruments tailored to this housing form.

The legal possibility of mobility has forced much of MH financing into areas regulated by consumer credit codes. However, it is clear that rules for credit transactions appropriate to stereos or refrigerators will not suffice for financing of a residence. The inappropriateness of MH inclusion in this category, therefore, has necessitated special exemptions to prevailing regulations. The solutions (if found at all) are characterized by an awkwardness that leaves all parties (lender, borrower, seller) less than content. The difficulties derive from attempting to bend a credit system to a purpose for which it is simply not suited.[5] Furthermore, the problems are exacerbated by the need to tailor solutions to the consumer code of each state.

Rather than attempting to fit MHs into the consumer credit system, a more elegant solution could be achieved by devising a mortgage instrument appropriate to MHs. (This is similar to the solution that was necessary to finance condominiums.) The creation of a model instrument would eliminate the idiosyncratic solutions now being attempted on a state-by-state basis. It would also guide attempts at solutions toward an MH-specific mechanism, a middle ground between personal and real property definitions that accurately represents the unique nature of this type of residence. In many respects the solutions for ownership recording and appropriate mortgage instrument are linked. A mechanism that guarantees a clear and continuous ownership record would provide a means for securing risk. In both instances the need is for an MH-specific solution, one which recognizes the dichotomous personal-real property nature of this type of residence.

Mortgage Terms

As with mortgage instruments, mortgage terms require a major change in orientation in order to effect a sensible solution. At present terms for both public and private sector lending are rooted in the historic perception of impermanence and absence of durability; changes occur incrementally from that base. Interest rates, maturities, and maximum allowable amounts are linked with the nature of construction, not market value. For federal programs this necessitates regular congressional review of programs, and modifications in authorizing statutes, a cumbersome process not sensitive to market fluctuations. Moreover, in the absence of systematic evidence regarding market behavior and comparative durability, it is not clear that there is a basis for objective determination of sensible mortgage maximums and maturities.[6]

To continue to restrict MH loan terms (especially mortgage maximums) following prior practices precludes offering MHs in housing markets under normal market conditions. A mortgage maximum based on structure type rather than size and location restricts MH sellers in possible market segments, since MH mortgage maximums typically are lower than for equivalently sized site-built homes. A shorter maturity and higher interest (either or in combination) means that buyers are paying higher monthly housing costs than they would for the same priced, site-built home.

If the differences in terms were based on clear and current actuarial evidence, the continuation of the practice would be easily supportable. However, evidence shows that the conventional wisdoms about lack of durability are not correct. Continued studies (especially of a comparative nature) would further clarify the issue. There is also some indication that risk exposure on MH loans is decreasing, probably a function of the expanding market share (with a concomitant upward movement in socioeconomic profile of MH occupants) resulting from greater sales of multi-section homes. Again, systematic and comparative studies would provide a better ground for determining appropriate loan terms.

Here the experience of the FHLBB is instructive. The Horton studies comparing risk exposure of S&Ls governed by the Bank Board, and those governed only by state regulation, found that the more stringent FHLBB regulations did not improve the risk exposure for federally regulated S&Ls. It is likely that many other conventional wisdoms would similarly prove to be unreliable guides for policy once subjected to serious scrutiny. It is important, therefore, that policy be rooted in supportable evidence.

Capital Availability

The issues of mortgage terms and capital availability are very much linked since both are currently approached on the premise that to treat MHs based on their structural properties is sound financial practice. It is clear that resulting legal definitions do necessitate certain unique treatment for the structural properties in terms of mortgage instruments. However, it is not clear, as suggested in the preceding section, that this distinction is useful for making financial judgments.

The difficulty in changing practices is that MHs have not had the freedom of the marketplace afforded other housing forms. Thus an accumulation of market-based evidence is lacking on which to structure new and different approaches to making capital available. Since financiers respond primarily to market-based evidence, they have an understandable initial hesitancy to make changes regarding MHs. What results is a Catch-22 situation, which can be countered only by focused study of evidence that reasonably reflects unrestricted MH market behavior. It may be that the experience of Oregon's veterans housing and housing revenue bond programs could provide such evidence. Another possibility would be MH performance in the California market, given changes in the legal and institutional context resulting from the recent statutory changes.

The possibilities are considerable for expansion of capital availability by each of the agencies with either direct or indirect financing programs. Resolution on the comparability issue could open up HUD's 203(b) loan program and its related secondary market activity. HUD has already recommended a number of technical changes in authorizing statute regarding use of cooperative and condominium financing tools (HUD, 1981). The Section 8 changes pending in the Congress in 1981 are a first step to attracting developer use of MHs in the Section 8-new program. Implementation of FmHA's MH program authority would increase financing availability. At the federal level an even greater source of increased capital availability would be expanded secondary market activities by the FNMA and FHLMC, as well as additional changes by the FHLBB toward equivalency in lending activity for MHs and other SFDs.[7]

An almost totally untapped source of capital is the network of state housing finance agencies. Even more than the agencies at the federal level, HFAs maintain conventional wisdoms toward MHs. Yet without exception they are able to operate using tax-free bonds because of authorizing language establishing a positive public purpose in their housing lending activities. Presumably, providing decent housing at reasonable cost meets tests of public purpose. Here the results of the comparability studies would be useful evidence in prompting HFA consideration of MHs in their various programs.

Following the same public purpose argument, a basis may exist for congressional creation of positive incentives in the private market for use of this housing. If in fact unit costs are lower than those of similar site-built units, then MHs can provide, using private sector mechanisms, a housing solution for a portion of the population that might otherwise turn to public resources or a less desirable solution to meet their housing needs. A number of possible incentive mechanisms to prompt housing activity generally have received attention and approbation, such as tax-free housing savings certificates. These or similar incentives can be specifically tailored as well to MHs.

Market Trends

Until the early to mid-1970s, the MH industry had a readily distinguishable share of the market, primarily resulting from the size and cost of units. MH residents tended to be either young couples in a first purchased residence, or older individuals or couples in a retirement residence. Assessed by typical socioeconomic standards, MH residents were in lower income categories, with relatively lower levels of educational achievement and blue-collar and similar employment. This market segment, which typically purchases single-section units (again for cost and size reasons), continues to be a major element of the MH buying population.

However, as the proportion of multisection units increases, and the average size of both single-section and all MH units increases, an increasing number of households in the middle-age range (30–55) are choosing to live in MHs. This group tends to have a somewhat different socioeconomic profile, with higher income, more education, a broader range of type of employment, and larger family size. This new market group is likely to increase, especially with the movement of some sections of the MH industry to real property development. Thus it is very likely that, as compared with the previously singular characteristics of the MH industry, the future will evolve at least two, and perhaps more, distinct and dissimilar parts.

The extent of industry differentiation will depend primarily on the degree of sophistication developed in market segmentation. As discussed in Chapter 4, market research within the industry is a relatively recent phenomenon. Given that MHs have not had free access to housing markets, more than usual creativity in approaches to market research for MHs will be necessary. Because MHs are rarely the first choice of housing consumers, it will be necessary to conduct special studies of the motivations of various current and/or potential consumer groups. Such studies will necessarily go beyond traditional market research techniques, which are premised on a buyer propensity to purchase, given proper prompting to a sale. They will also have to understand the institutional dynamics that influence a consumer's attraction to a substantive decision area, a necessary antecedent to even contemplating a purchase decision.[8]

The Elderly Market

An example of the sort of detailed analysis necessary to understand market possibilities is the choice of MHs by the elderly, who are becoming a much larger proportion of the American population. While the elderly have tended to be MH purchasers, the number of the elderly population actually purchasing MHs has not kept pace with their increasing numbers in the nation.

MHs in parks have been the typical choice of an elderly MH buyer. Is this choice a sound one for today's elderly population? What might be evidence pertinent to this question?

Two characteristics of the elderly population are important. First, they are financially vulnerable. The amount and sources of income for this group are relatively fixed, providing little flexibility to respond to the assaults of inflation, especially as it affects major fixed expenses such as shelter. Second, the lives of older people—physically, socially, psychologically, locationally—are becoming increasingly complex and without precedent in personal, family, or societal experience.

As presented in most marketing efforts by the MH industry, MHs are efficient dwelling units, low in cost to operate and easy to maintain. The HUD Code provides certain assurances of construction quality and occupant safety. Unit ownership by occupants, which is the norm in MH parks, increases the potential for a responsible citizenry generally attributed to areas of high home ownership. Because MH parks have relatively high densities for SFD areas, the resultant unit and occupant closeness increases the potential for social interaction. The single park owner provides a common focal point for park residents, creating an additional possibility for social cohesion.

The attributes of MHs and MH parks appear positive in terms of the shelter, financial, and social needs of older people. But because not all older people are the same, many forms of the MH and MH park may be necessary to meet the housing needs of this group. Among topics that would aid in matching MH and MH park opportunities with the diverse housing needs of older persons are the following:

1. Living Arrangements and Style: An older person living in an MH park has typically located there at or in anticipation of retirement. This move generally involves a few to many hundreds of miles from the previous housing unit, as well as a spatial distance from extended family. While propinquity may create community, it is not a necessary outcome. Some prompting of community interaction, tailored to the partic-

ular residents attracted to a given area, may be needed.

2. Demographic Changes: The profile of possible older persons attracted to MHs and MH parks is changing. In particular tax provisions allowing a one-time $125,000 capital gains exemption places this group in a different financial situation than that to which they are accustomed, at least on sale of the prior residence. Special attention to the consequences of these demographic dynamics is appropriate.

3. Private Sector Service Delivery: MH parks have a tradition of providing a variety of services (primarily recreational) as part of the amenities package. It is probable that the range of those services will need to expand, notably to include medical and personal security concerns. It may well be that some movement in the direction of quasipublic support and/or provision of some or all services in a park is appropriate.

Legal Topics

Although MHs are an integral part of the country's housing stock, their unique structural characteristics and the heritage of mobility yield a number of areas with unresolved legal issues. Among such issues are the relative legal rights when unit and land are in different ownership, the appropriate approaches to development incentives and controls, and sensible structuring of tax treatment at state and local levels. The following sections briefly discuss each of these issues.

Legal Rights of Unit and Land Owners

A substantial number of MH owners do not own the land on which their unit is located. Most of these units are in MH parks, though some are on leased land. Although both the unit and land owners have a substantial investment in location-specific property, no developed body of law provides guidance on the rights of each. Although tenant-landlord law typically is invoked, the precedents are in many respects inappropriate because the MH residents own their units and only rent the space on which they are located.

The problems resulting from the absence of sound practice and precedent are often tragic in their dimensions. Many result from MH park residents having right to their space on a tenancy-at-will or short-term lease basis. The sale of the park property for other purposes, always a possibility if the land is in a commercial zone, will result in forced relocation, often on short notice. This problem is especially acute in older MH parks.

Although many states have statutes governing some aspects of MH park owner and resident relationships, they tend to be based on tenant/landlord grounds, with the attendant assumptions of transiency. Whereas such statutes were important in constraining a range of unreasonable practices of an earlier time, they are not adequate for the contemporary task of establishing relative property rights in what is a unique and containing component of housing markets.

Development Incentives and Controls

As discussed in Chapter 5, most treatment of MHs at the local level has had a premise of control, even exclusion. Arbitrary exclusion and controls are obviously no longer sound policy and are not being sustained by the courts, as evidenced in the *Robinson Township* v. *Knoll* decision. The potential that MHs hold for meeting the housing needs of various segments of the population will require changes in state statutes and local ordinances, so that appropriate legal frameworks exist for both development incentives and controls.

The California statute established a set of contraints on MH controls in local zoning ordinances, and provided for state review to ascertain conformance with the statutory requirements. Massachusetts is considering a similar approach via executive order. State development assistance funds would not be granted to communities which are determined to be unreasonably restrictive of new housing. Among possible evidence of exclusionary practices would be implicit or explicit exclusion of manufactured housing.

In addition to legal mechanisms which constrain local exclusionary practices, it is important to provide mechanisms which offer incentives for sensible use of MHs. The following two examples are indicative of how incentives tailored to the unique nature of MHs can solve particular housing needs of communities. The first involves energy boom-towns, which experience sudden, large increases in housing demand, with peak demand exceeding predicted level demand by a significant proportion. Zoning code provisions allowing for time-constrained two-unit use (one being a non-affixed MH) of a one-unit lot would have several beneficial effects. It would not be necessary to construct infrastructure beyond the spatial area expected to handle level housing demand (though somewhat higher capacity for water and sewer would be necessary to manage peak demand). The use of MHs to house at least the differential between level and peak (as well as that portion of basic demand that would select MHs independently) would eliminate temporary in-migration of the housing construction labor force needed for the number of housing units represented by the MHs if they were site-built homes. MHs also have a shorter time between need identification and occupancy, and thus can accommodate the ebbs and flows in demand more rapidly. Finally, if energy boom-towns are a sequential phenomenon, individuals who move from one to the next to be part of the work force at peak demand can take their homes with them, making the mobility of MHs a useful attribute.

The second example of how an MH-linked development incentive can respond to special housing needs involves the elderly. Again, it involves providing an increase in lot density from one to two units. In this case the additional unit is for one or two elderly persons, often but not necessarily members of the extended family of the owner-occupant of the initial unit on the lot. The concept is currently used in Australia and is referred to as "granny flats." The additional unit provides for freedom and independence of the elderly occupants, but also provides a close-by support system.

Tax Treatment

The ambiguities in legal definition of MHs yield equally confusing tax treatment. The problems associated with determination of value were discussed earlier and derive in many ways from the legal definition dilemmas. The initial personal property definition has meant that MHs are subject to sales tax. Most states tax the full sales price, thus taxing construction and sales labor as well as materials. This differs from tax treatment for site-built houses, for which only materials are taxed. To provide equalization in treatment, some states have provided that sales tax is applicable to only a fixed proportion of sales price. Taxation of MHs in parks, and the park itself, will continue to be a complicated matter, since ownership of unit and land is separate. (The one exception is condominium or cooperative ownership of the park by the residents, though the assessment difficulties associated with non-affixation might well remain.) It may well be that a tax letter arrangement, would be more appropriate for MH parks. The specially determined tax liability would account for the lower demand on public services of MH parks, as well as provide a mechanism to deal with the value determination difficulties.

A final tax area requiring some legal resolution is the treatment of existing unit owners when shifts from existing to new tax methods are made. The California precedent is instructive since it accounted for the impacts that real estate taxation would have on those who made their MH choice on the assumption of the previous personal property approach. A "hold-harmless" mechanism was devised so that MH owners to whom taxation on the previous basis was important could remain in that category. California requires annual licensing of the MH unit by these owners. A lapse in licensing or a sale of the unit automatically moves it into the real property taxation category.

Notes

1. Approaches to dealing with these topics have a particular dilemma in that differentiation of housing forms (MH from site-built houses, for example) necessitates asserting some premise of difference. This very statement of difference allows a thought process that rank orders the housing types in terms of quality, regardless of whether the differentiation dealt with issue. What then occurs is the imposition of a normative conclusion that a higher rank is "better" and a lower rank "worse," even if all housing types ranked meet or exceed objective standards of acceptability. This error is similar to the statistically invalid procedure of summing nominal or ordinal data.
2. An important consideration in comparative studies is longitudinal as well as one-time comparisons. The DOD comparisons described in Chapter 6 are the first such direct comparison with a longitudinal feature. Unfortunately, because the construction code is military, the direct transference of the outcomes of the analysis to private market housing will be more difficult to achieve.
3. Recent MH park developments by dealers and the emerging direct development activity of manufacturers are the exceptions to this statement.

4. In 1978 the American Association of Motor Vehicle Administrators adopted a Uniform Manufacturer's Certificate of Origin. This form, which is specially printed with security features by three licensed companies, is designed for motor vehicle use. States requiring titling typically require use of this form.

5. For example, in 1981 the Texas legislature enacted a bill that modified the state's consumer credit code to provide for adjustable rates in MH loans governed by that code. What is notable about the bill is the nature and number of contortions necessary to fit a prevailing shelter loan practice (adjustable rates) into consumer loan regulations.

6. It is interesting to note that HUD stipulated to its researchers a 40-year useful life for FHA-insured single-family dwellings as its comparative base for durability assessment of MHs. No structural evidence was cited for this stipulation, only FHA insuring practices.

7. A paper prepared by the Coordinating Council on MH Finance for the Development Choices for the '80s Council presents an extensive discussion of possible changes in financing (Coordinating Council, 1980).

8. For a discussion of the theory and methods of institutional analysis, and an example of how institutional forces guide propensity to contemplate something different from the ordinary in the housing arena, see Nutt-Powell et al., 1979.

Appendix

CODE COMPARISONS

Comparison of Construction Standards: HUD MH Code vs. BOCA Single-Family Dwelling Code (1978)

Structural Design Requirements (Pennsylvania Zone)	HUD Code	BOCA Code	HUD Code MH Standard Requirements Same-Less-More Than BOCA
Live Loads (Minimum)			
Wind load	Horizontal, 15 psf.	Horizontal, 10 psf.	More
Roof load	Snow/Live, 20 psf.	Snow/Live, 20 psf.	Same
Floor distributed load	Live, 40 psf.	Live, 40 psf.	Same
Load Deflections (Maximum)			
Floors	Unplastered, 1/240 span.	Unplastered, 1/240 span.	Same
Roof	Unplastered, 1/180 span.	Unplastered, 1/180 span.	Same
Windstorm Protection			
Sliding and overturning	Designed provisions for support and anchoring.	Standard methods.	N/A
Resistance to weather	Exterior covering materials and construction duly tested for resistance to elements and use.	Exterior covering materials and construction duly tested for resistance to elements and use.	Same
Structural Tests	Assemblies not subject to engineering design are tested.	Assemblies not subject to engineering design are tested.	Same
Fire Safety			
Interior finish	Flame spread rating not exceeding 200.	Flame spread rating not exceeding 200.	Same
Furnace, water heater and cooking range areas	Special protection with gypsum/asbestos/sheet metal.	No special provisions for fire protection.	More

Smoke detection	1 smoke detector for each bedroom area.	1 smoke detector in each sleeping area.	Same
Exit Facilities (Minimum)			
Exterior door	2	1	More
Egress	1 in every bedroom.	1 in every bedroom.	Same
Space Planning (Minimum Requirements)			
Overall floor area	Not specified.	Not specified.	Same
Sizes of rooms	Living room, 150 sq ft; Double bedroom, 70 sq ft	Living room, 150 sq ft; Bedrooms, 70 sq ft	Same
Ceiling height	7 ft	7½ ft	Less
Hallways	28 in	36 in	Less
Light and Ventilation (Minimum)			
Glazed area	8%	8%	Same
Unobstructed area	4%	4%	Same
Mechanical ventilation	Habitable, 2 air change/hr.; Bath, 5 air change/hr.	Habitable, 2 air change/hr.; Bath, 5 air change/hr.	Same
Thermal Protection	Equipment and insulation to provide 70°F inside in winter.	Equipment and insulation to provide 70°F inside in winter.	Same
Plumbing			
Material	Nationally accepted standards (ANSI, ASTM, FS, others).	Nationally accepted standards.	Same
Construction and system	Accepted methods.	Accepted methods (almost identical).	Same

Comparison of Construction Standards (cont.)

Structural Design Requirements (Pennsylvania Zone)	HUD Code	BOCA Code	HUD Code MH Standard Requirements Same-Less-More Than BOCA
Tests and inspections	Water system, drainage and vent system, and fixtures are tested.	Water system, drainage and vent system, and fixtures are tested (almost same tests are applicable).	Same
Electrical			
Material	Acceptable under NEC.	Acceptable under NEC.	Same
Construction and system	NEC.	NEC.	Same
Electrical tests	Dielectric, continuity operational, polarity tests/NEC.	NEC.	Same
Transportation	Designed to fully withstand the transportation shocks and vibrations.	N/A.	N/A
Design Evaluations	Designed by professional engineers/architects and checked by independent professionals.	Site-built residences not necessarily designed and checked by professionals.	More
Inspections During Construction	Inspected by independent inspectors and public officials.	Local inspectors.	More

SOURCE: Goel, Yash P. 1978. Report to Commonwealth of Pennsylvania, Dept. of Community Affairs, Bureau of Housing and Development, Division of Industrialized and Mobile Housing.

Comparison of Design Criteria, Single-Family Dwelling, HUD MH Code vs. Uniform Building Code

Design Elements	Design Criteria	
	Federal MH Construction and Safety Standards	UBC 1976 UPC 1976 NEC 1978
Zoning		
Occupancy	One-family dwelling	R-3 (residential single family)
Type of construction	Per local jurisdictions	V-N (wood frame construction combustible)
Fire zone	Per local jurisdictions	3 (residential)
Location on property	Per local jurisdictions	Over 3′ to property line for unprotected opening in walls
Structural Design Loads		
Roof live load	20 psf*	20 psf*
Wind load, horizontal	15 psf	15 psf
Wind load, uplift	9 psf	11.25 psf
Floor live load	40 psf	40 psf
Horizontal load on interior walls	5 psf	None specified
Live load deflections		
Floor	L/240	L/240
Side wall	L/180	L/120
Roof/ceiling	L/180	L/180
Test load requirements	2.5 × LL	2.5 × LL
Architectural Design—Building Planning		
Glazed area	8% of floor area	10% of floor area
Vent area	4% of floor area	5% of floor area
Minimum room size:		
One room	150 sq ft	150 sq ft
Bedroom (2 persons)	70 sq ft	70 sq ft
Bedroom (min.)	50 sq ft	70 sq ft
Minimum room dimension	5 ft	7 ft
Closet depth (required in each bedroom)	22 in	None specified
Toilet compartment	30 in wide with 21 in clear	30 in wide with 24 in clear
Hall width	28 in	None specified
Ceiling height—general	7 ft	7 ft, 6 in
Exterior wall covering	Weather-resistive and corrosion-resistant fasteners	Prescribes minimum materials and fasteners

Comparison of Design Criteria, Single-Family Dwelling (cont.)

	Design Criteria	
Design Elements	Federal MH Construction and Safety Standards	UBC 1976 UPC 1976 NEC 1978
Fire Safety		
Exit doors	2	1
Specify exterior door locations	Yes	No
Bedroom egress window:	Yes	Yes
Minimum size	5 sq ft	5.7 sq ft
Minimum sill height	36 in	44 in
Furnace compartment lining	Gyp. bd. + 25 FS max	Not specified
Water heater compartment lining	Gyp. bd. + 25 FS max	Not specified
Furnace/water heater compartment—sealed from living area environment	Required or use sealed combustion appliance	Not required
Kitchen range back wall	Gyp. bd. + 50 FS max	Not specified
Protect cabinets above range	Yes	Yes
Smoke detector(s)	Yes	Yes
Fire blocking in walls	8 ft	10 ft
Flamespread in living areas		
Walls	200 or less (Class III)	Class III**
Ceiling	200 or less (Class III)	Class III**
Thermal Energy Conservation		
Condensation control		
Walls	Vapor barrier	Vapor barrier
Ceiling	Vapor barrier	Not specified
Air infiltration control	Specified	Not specified
Maximum heat loss	Specified	Not specified
Double glazing or storm windows	Mandatory	Not mandatory
Requires listed appliances	Yes	Yes
Interior heated to 70°F	Required	Required

Comparison of Design Criteria, Single-Family Dwelling (cont.)

	Design Criteria	
Design Elements	*Federal MH Construction and Safety Standards*	*UBC 1976 UPC 1976 NEC 1978*
Plumbing		
Hot and cold supply		
Pipe sizing	No. of fixtures	No. of fixture units
Plastic pipe	Yes	No
DWV system		
Drain pipe size	Comparable	Comparable
Horizontal wet vent	Yes	No
Cleanouts	Over 45° each, 360° total	135° total
Listed materials and fixtures	Yes	Yes
Gas piping	Comparable	Comparable
Vertical wet venting	Yes	Yes
Electrical		
Require listed material and devices	Yes	Yes
Aluminum wire in branch circuits	Not permitted	Permitted
Receptacle locations	Comparable	Comparable
Load calculations	Comparable	Comparable
Separate neutral and ground on appliances and equipment	Yes	No
Site Development		
Grading	Per local jurisdictions	Specified
Foundation design	Per local jurisdictions	Specified
Anchorage to foundation	Specified	Specified

SOURCE: Fleetwood Enterprises, 1978.

* Building official or home manufacturer may adopt higher loads to meet local conditions.

** Not applicable to finishes in kitchen or bathroom.

Comparison of HUD MH Code and UBC Modular Code

Item	*HUD MH Code*	*UBC Modular Code*
Frames	The frame is considered to be part of the floor system.	Omit entire frame. Use modular returnable carrier.
Floor system	Standard is performance oriented, and structural requirements are based on calculations or tests. Prescriptive structural requirements are not specified. Details below are typical mobile home construction.	
	Floor joists at 16″ o.c.	Floor joists at 16″ o.c.
	Single-rim members.	Double rim members.
	2 × 6 floor joist on 24 ft and 28 ft wide models.	2 × 8 SPF#2 or better floor joists on 24 ft wide. 2 × 10 SPF#2 or better floor joist on 28 ft wide.
	5/8 in particle board NPA 1-73 D2 or D3 full width.	Floor decking to be 5/8 in particle board 2-B-II. 3/4 in × 4 × 12 Group 3 underlayment grade and blunt edge. 5/8 in × 4 × 8 T & G Group 3 underlayment.
	Bottom board material.	Bottom board with crawl space only. Omit insulation when unit has full basement (7 ft-0 in height minimum).
	Floor load LL 40 psf.	Floor load LL 40 psf.
Exterior walls	2 × 3 at 16 in o.c. cheater wall 2 × 4 at 16 in o.c.	2 × 4 at 16 in o.c.
	Single 1x top plate exterior wall and marriage wall.	Double 2x top plate exterior and marriage wall.
	Single 1x bottom plate.	Single 2x bottom plate.
	Header requirements: Lauan headers Solid headers	Header requirements (SPF): 32″ opening—2 2 × 4 stud grade 48″ opening—2 2 × 6 #3 or better 64″ opening—2 2 × 6 #2 or better All headers require 1/2″ spacer.

Comparison of HUD MH Code and UBC Modular Code (cont.)

Item	HUD MH Code	UBC Modular Code
	Jack studs only per window opening.	Window jambs require jack studs.
	Corner bracing not required.	Corner bracing requires 50 ft of galv. strap 1-1/4 in × 16 ga. or 1 × 4 let in brace (exterior structural sheathing may replace this requirement). Must meet seismic loads.
	Wind load 15–25 psf.	Wind Load: 15–30 psf.
Interior walls	Nonload bearing walls 1 × 3 min. 16 in o.c. 1 × 3 top and bottom plate. Walls fastened to ceiling at rafter chord or 1 × 3 nailer at joist or to floor decking.	Nonload bearing walls 2 × 3 at 16 in o.c. minimum, 2x top and bottom plates. Walls fastened to ceiling at rafter chord or 2 × 3 block at 24 in o.c. and fastened to floor at joist or 2 × 4 blocking at 24 in o.c.
	Load bearing walls single 1x top and bottom plate, can use a post support system on marriage walls. Fastened to ceiling member and to a floor joist or member	Load bearing walls double 2x top plate, single 2x bottom plate, continuous marriage wall. Fastened to ceiling same as nonload bearing wall and fastened to floor at double joist.
	Shear walls: Zone 1–15 psf; Zone 2–25 psf. 2 × 3 minimum at 16 in o.c. restricted fastening. Fastened to ceiling at rafter chord and at floor to a floor joist. Lagged to floor at ends.	All walls are calculated for 15–30 psf, and must meet seismic loads.
Roofs	Roof loads: 20 psf and up.	Roof load: 20 psf and up.
	All rafters are tested and certified.	Engineered trussed rafters required with minimum 2 × 3 chords and verticals. Bottom chord must be calculated to withstand LL 10 psf.
	Galv. metal roof standard with option of shingles 235# with 30# felt.	Shingles standard 235# with 30# felt.

Comparison of HUD MH Code and UBC Modular Code (cont.)

Item	*HUD MH Code*	*UBC Modular Code*
	Venting of attic area required for shingle roofs min. to 1/300 of area.	Venting of attic area required at 1/300 of area.
	2 × 3 look-out support members.	Gable framing at end wall requires 2 × 4 ladder construction.
	Attic access not required.	Attic access 22 in × 30 in if minimum 30 in clear head room in attic.
	2 to 12 pitch minimum with shingle roof, none with metal roof.	3 to 12 pitch minimum.
Exterior sheathing	Not required.	Structural sheathing or corner bracing.
	Aluminum panel siding minimum optional Masonite hardboard, or house-type lap siding.	Subsheathing required or 15# felt, or structural finished siding. 5/8 in structural facia (Upson) required. 3/8 in structural soffit (Upson) required.
Plumbing	Optional.	Supply shutoff at all fixtures.
	Auto vents are approved to be used where permissible by code.	No auto vents, 1-1/2 in diameter vents all fixtures.
	Not required.	3 in main vent at 3 in drain.
	Optional.	Hose bib to outside required.
	CPVC or poly-supply lines are approved and listed as well as galvanized steel, Type K, L, or M copper tubing. ABS or PVC drain line.	Galvanized and copper supply lines only. ABS or PVC drain line OK.
Electrical	Materials acceptable under NEC.	Materials acceptable under NEC.
	Construction and system per the MH Federal Standards and the NEC.	Construction and system per NEC.

Comparison of HUD MH Code and UBC Modular Code (cont.)

Item	HUD MH Code	UBC Modular Code
Space planning (minimum)	Overall floor area is not specified.	Overall floor area is not specified.
	Room sizes: living area, 150 sq ft; bedrooms, 50 sq ft; double bedroom, 70 sq ft; plus 50 sq ft for each person in excess of two.	living area, 150 sq ft; bedrooms, 70 sq ft.
Light and ventilation (minimum)	Glazed area, 8%; unobstructed, 4%; Mechanical ventilation: habitable, 2 air change/hr; bath, 5 air change/hr.	Glazed area, 10% of room area (10 sq ft min.); unobstructed, 5% of room area (5 sq ft min.); Mechanical ventilation: habitable, 2 air change/hr.; bath, 5 air change/hr.
Fire safety	One smoke detector protecting each bedroom area.	One smoke detector protecting each bedroom area.
	Interior finish: flame spread rating not exceeding 200.	Interior finish: flame spread rating not exceeding 200.
	Furnace, water heater, and cooking range areas: special protection with gypsum, asbestos, or sheet metal.	Furnace, water heater, and cooking range areas: no special provisions for fire protection.
Miscellaneous	Interior wall finish minimum: 5/32" paneling	Interior wall finish minimum: 1/4" paneling
	Two exterior doors. One must be 32" clear opening.	Two exterior doors. 34" clear opening.
	Windows to comply with federal standards.	Windows to comply with ASHRAE 90 for infiltration.
		Heat loss and insulation system change.
	Insulation varies to comply with code max. coefficient factor for 0° outside temperature (Zone 1) and −20° (Zone 2).	Min. insulation. R-25 roof; R-14 walls; R-11 floors (unheated crawl space).
	All heat loss per 501BM or ASHRAE	All heat loss per ASHRAE 90 per degree day requirements of area of installation.

Comparison of HUD MH Code and UBC Modular Code (cont.)

Item	HUD MH Code	UBC Modular Code
	Not required.	6 in branch ducts required.
	One egress window in every bedroom.	One egress window in every bedroom.
	Furnace and water heater shall be installed to provide for the complete separation of the combustion system from the interior atmosphere (or sealed combustion).	No special provisions required.
Installation (foundation)	Have a pier support system with tie-downs or permanent foundation.	Permanent foundation.

SOURCE: Guerdon Industries.

Comparison of HUD MH Code and SBCC Residential Standards

HUD	*SBCC*

ITEM 1: PLANS AND SPECIFICATIONS

Section 3282.203(a) through (g)

Extensive plans and specifications are mandatory for each MH production covering chassis design, structural, electrical, hvac and plumbing. These plans must be approved by an architectural or engineering agency that is approved by HUD.

Section 105.3

Plans and specifications are only required at the request of the building official and need not be approved by an engineer or architect.

ITEM 2: QUALITY CONTROL

Section 3282.203(c)

Requires a mandatory quality control program and qualified personnel to administer it. The quality control program must be approved by a HUD-approved agency. It is also mandatory that each MH still be inspected by both the quality control personnel and the state inspection agency.

None.

ITEM 3: MANUFACTURING CERTIFICATION REQUIREMENTS

Section 3282.205(a) through (b)(8)

Requires the inspection agency to certify that the manufacturer is capable of building MHs that conform to approved design and to the standards and are inspected in accordance with the approved quality control program by the manufacturer's quality control personnel on a continuing basis.

None.

ITEM 4: INSPECTIONS

Section 3282.204(a) through (e)

Requires that each MH be inspected in at least one stage of production by an inspection agency approved by

All phases of construction, electrical and plumbing to be inspected by the local authority having jurisdiction.

Comparison of HUD and SBCC Residential Standards (cont.)

HUD	*SBCC*

HUD to assure that the manufacturer continues to build all MHs to comply to the approved design, standards, and approved quality control program, and that all violations found are reported and corrected.

In addition to inspecting each MH   None.
in at least one phase of construction, the inspectors must inspect all test equipment at least once a month.

ITEM 5: STRUCTURAL

Section 3280.104(a)

Ceiling heights: Minimum height 7'-0"

Ceiling heights: Minimum height 7'-6"

Section 3280.110(a)(b)(c)

1. Single occupancy bedroom minimum of 50 sq. ft.
2. Designed for 2—70 sq. ft. plus an additional 50 sq. ft. for each person over 2.

2. At least one room 150 sq. ft.

3. Living space of 150 sq. ft.

Section 3280.304(a)

All dimension and board lumber shall not exceed 19% moisture content at time of installation. (The manufacturer must provide the necessary testing equipment and perform this test to comply with this requirement.)

Section 1700.6

Requires all lumber and plywood members, including pressure treated, 2 inches and less in thickness, shall contain not more than 19% moisture content at time of installation.

Section 3280.305

Structural load requirements:
1. Floor—40 lb. per sq. ft.
2. Wall—wind load 125 mph winds

Section 1203.1

1. Floor—40 lb. per sq. ft.
2. Wall—wind load varies depending on location in state—110, 120, 130 mph

3. Roof—20 lb. per sq. ft. In comparable locations, 30 lb. per sq. ft. in northern states

3. Roof—20 lb. per sq. ft.

Comparison of HUD and SBCC Residential Standards (cont.)

HUD	SBCC

Section 3280.112
 	
Toilet compartment
    30″ width
    21″ clear space in front
	None.

ITEM 6: LIFE SAFETY

HUD	SBCC
Section 3280.106(a)(b)(c) 1. Exit facilities require an *approved* egress window or door in all bedrooms. 2. Height of egress window from floor: 36″. 3. Operating device for opening egress window must not be more than 60″ from floor.	*Section 1.1104.5* 1. Requires at least one operable window or door *approved* for emergency egress or rescue. 2. Height of egress window from floor: 44″. 3. None.
Section 3280.105 Requires a minimum of 2 exterior doors located remote from each other.	Requires 1 exterior door.
Section 3280.106(a)(b)(c) 1. Size of egress window, minimum of 5 sq. ft. 2. Minimum clear opening, 22″.	1. Size of egress window, minimum of 5 sq. ft. grade floor, above grade 5.7 sq. ft. 2. Minimum height opening 24″, minimum width opening 20″.
Section 3280.203(a) through (b) Flamespread limitations: 1. Interior finish of all walls and partitions must have a minimum flamespread rating of 200 (Class C). 2. Ceilings—minimum of 200 flamespread (Class C). 3. Furnace and water heater compartments—walls, ceilings and doors must have minimum of 25 flamespread (Class A).	Flamespread limitations: 1. Flamespread rating of 200 for interior finish. 2. Flamespread minimum of 200. 3. None.
Section 3280.203(a) through (b) 4. Combustible kitchen cabinet doors, exposed bottoms and end panels must have a maximum flamespread rating of 200.	4. None.

Comparison of HUD and SBCC Residential Standards (cont.)

HUD	*SBCC*
5. Exposed interior finishes adjacent to cooking range minimum flame-spread rating of 50.	5. None.

Section 3280.204(a)

Requires the bottom and sides of combustible kitchen cabinets over cooking ranges to be protected with 3/8" gypsum or the equivalent covered with not less than 26 gauge sheet metal.	None.

Section 3280.206(a)	*Section 705*
Requires fire-stopping materials to be minimum 1" nominal lumber or equivalent at all draft openings.	Requires 2" nominal lumber for fire-stopping.

Section 3280.208(a) through (d)	*Section 1127*
Fire detection equipment required:	
1. At least one approved smoke detector; 2 are required if split bedroom arrangement.	1. One smoke detector to be installed.
2. Location of smoke detectors to be between living area and bedrooms in hallways, 5" to 7" from ceiling.	2. Installed in accordance with manufacturer's installation instructions.
3. Detector to be attached to outlet box and connected by permanent wiring method.	3. Battery operated detectors allowed.

ITEM 7: PLUMBING

Section 3280.601 through 3280.612 (d)	*Standard Plumbing Code* Same as HUD.
All plumbing systems basically same except residential requires a minimum 2" main vent where a 1½" main vent is allowed in MHs.	

Comparison of HUD and SBCC Residential Standards (cont.)

HUD	*SBCC*

ITEM 8: ELECTRICAL

Section 3280.801 through 3280.816

Currently the 1975 National Electrical Code is used for code compliance on MHs.	Currently the 1978 National Electrical Code is enforced.

SOURCE: Guerdon Industries.

BIBLIOGRAPHY

Automation in Housing and Systems Building News (AIH/SBN). 1980. "AIH/SBN Top 100 Home Producers Report Shows '79 a Great Year," August, pp. 18–20+.

Banking. 1978. "Better Way to Appraise Mobile Homes," October, pp. 120–122.

Bernhardt, Arthur D., with the assistance of Susan A. Comando and Herbert B. Zien. 1980. *Building Tomorrow: The Mobile/Manufactured Housing Industry*. Cambridge, Mass.: MIT Press.

Beverly, William M. 1980. "Used MHs: Finding the Real Value," *Manufactured Housing DEALER*, pp. 34–35.

Budnick, Edward K., and David P. Klein. 1979. *Mobile Home Fire Studies: Summary and Recommendations*. Washington, D.C.: U.S. Department of Housing and Urban Development.

Bureau of the Census (AHS). 1978. *1976 Annual Housing Survey*. Washington, D.C.: U.S. Department of Commerce.

Carr, Judith M. 1980. "Candlewood Glen Lights the Future," *Manufactured Housing DEALER*, October, pp. 62–65.

Coordinating Council. 1980. *HUD Code Manufactured Housing and Development Choices for the '80s*. Washington, D.C.: Coordinating Council on Manufactured Housing Finance.

Danner, Pamela Beck. 1981. "HUD Notice Qualifies Industry for Financing under 203(b)," Mobile/Manufactured Home MERCHANDISER, August, p. 32.

DC '80s. 1981. Report of the Council on Development Choices for the '80s. Washington, D.C.: U.S. Department of Housing and Urban Development.

Fleetwood Enterprises. 1978. *Manufactured Home Buyer Profile*. Tustin, Cal.: Product Management Co.

FNMA. 1979. *A Guide to Fannie Mae*. Washington, D.C.: Federal National Mortgage Association.

————. 1981a. *Executive Summaries of Mortgage Programs*. Washington, D.C.: Federal National Mortgage Association.

————. 1981b. *Conventional Projects: Status of FNMA Acceptance*. Washington, D.C.: Federal National Mortgage Association.

FTC. 1980. *Mobile Home Sales and Service: Final Staff Report to the Federal Trade Commission and Proposed Trade Regulation Rule.* August. Washington, D.C.: Federal Trade Commission.

Furlong, Michael, and Thomas E. Nutt-Powell. 1980. *Development Controls for Mobile-Component Housing: A Ten-Year Review of the Law.* September. Cambridge, Mass.: Joint Center for Urban Studies.

Gates, Howard. 1980*a. Comparison of Fire Risk in Mobile Homes and Site-Built Homes.* Arlington, Va.: Manufactured Housing Institute.

————. 1980*b. Manufactured Homes and Site-Built Houses: Comparison of HUD Standards, Eligibility for FHA Loans, and Loan Costs to Purchasers.* Arlington, Va.: Manufactured Housing Institute.

Geomet. 1980. *An Evaluation of Formaldehyde Problems in Residential Mobile Homes.* Washington, D.C.: U.S. Department of Housing and Urban Development.

GNMA. 1980. *Government National Mortgage Association Mortgage-Backed Securities Guide.* Washington, D.C.: Department of Housing and Urban Development.

Horton, Joseph. 1979. "Mobile Home Lending: Its Relative Safety and Special Problems," *FHLBB Journal,* March, pp. 14–17.

HUD. 1978. *Final Report of the Task Force on Housing Costs.* Washington, D.C.: U.S. Department of Housing and Urban Development.

————. 1980. *Fourth Report to Congress on Mobile Homes.* Washington, D.C.: U.S. Department of Housing and Urban Development.

————. 1981. *Policy and Program Recommendations to Encourage Land Ownership in Mobile Home Communities.* Washington, D.C.: U.S. Department of Housing and Urban Development.

Kovacs, William D., and Felix Y. Yokel. 1979. *Soil and Rock Anchors for Mobile Homes—A State-of-the-Art Report.* Washington, D.C.: National Bureau of Standards.

Krueger, Gordon P., and L. Bogue Sandberg. 1979. *Durability of Structural Adhesives for Use in the Manufacture of Mobile Homes.* Washington, D.C.: U.S. Department of Housing and Urban Development.

Legislative Study Commission. 1980. *Report and Recommendations of the Mobile Home Study Commission.* Trenton: State of New Jersey.

Malnight, Jim. 1980. "Mobile Homes Appreciate in Value," *Manufactured Housing DEALER,* January, pp. 16–18.

Manufactured Housing DEALER. 1980. "Changing Old Images at Tierra del Sol," October, pp. 32–33.

MHI. 1976. *Manufactured Home Financing.* Arlington, Va.: Manufactured Housing Institute.

————. 1980. *Manufactured Home Financing: 1978–1979.* Arlington, Va.: Manufactured Housing Institute.

————. 1981*a. Quick Facts about the Manufactured Housing Industry.* Arlington, Va.: Manufactured Housing Institute.

————. 1981*b*. *Manufactured Home Financing in 1980.* Arlington, Va.: Manufactured Housing Institute.

Mobile/Manufactured Home MERCHANDISER. 1989. "Broker Sells Resales as "Real" Estates," September, pp. 24–26.

————. 1981*a*. "Resale Market Requires Real Estate Techniques," February, p. 24.

————. 1981*b*. "G-P Develops Formaldehyde Standards in Plants," May, p. 56.

NAHM. 1980. *Guide to Manufactured Homes.* Falls Church, Va.: National Association of Home Manufacturers.

New Hampshire Housing Commission. 1980. *New Hampshire Mobile Home Study.* June. Concord, N.H.: Office of State Planning.

NCSBCS. *Monthly Mobile Home Statistics.* Herndon, Virginia: National Conference of States on Building Codes and Standards.

Nutt-Powell, Thomas E., et al. 1979. *Solar Heating and Cooling of Housing: Five Institutional Analysis Case Studies.* Cambridge, Mass.: MIT Energy Laboratory.

Nutt-Powell, Thomas E., and Michael Furlong. 1980*a*. *Mobile-Component Housing and Solar Energy: The Possibilities.* April. Cambridge, Mass.: Joint Center for Urban Studies.

Nutt-Powell, Thomas E., and Michael Furlong with Christopher Pilkington. 1980*b*. *The States and Manufactured Housing.* June. Cambridge, Mass.: Joint Center for Urban Studies.

Nutt-Powell, Thomas E., and Michael Furlong. 1980*c*. *Mobile-Component Housing: A Literature Review and Annotated Bibliography.* August, Cambridge, Mass.: Joint Center for Urban Studies.

Owens-Corning. 1978. *Barriers to Greater Sales Growth: An Investigation of Consumer Shelter Decision-Making as it Impacts the Mobile Home Industry.* Toledo, Ohio: Owens-Corning Fiberglas Corporation.

Perry, Grady. 1977. "Speech," *Federal Home Loan Bank Board Journal,* March, pp. 3–6.

Roode, Roger L. 1980. "Mobile Home Appraisals: Who Needs Them?" *Manufactured Housing DEALER,* June 14, pp. 16–18.

Science Applications, Inc. 1979*a*. *Mobile Home Heating, Cooling and Fuel Burning Systems Test Report.* Washington, D.C.: U.S. Department of Housing and Urban Development.

————. 1979*b*. *Mobile Home Thermal Envelope Systems Test Report.* Washington, D.C.: U.S. Department of Housing and Urban Development.

Southwest Research Institute (SWRI). 1979. *Mobile Home Research: Transportation and Site-Installation.* Washington, D.C.: U.S. Department of Housing and Urban Development.

————. 1980. *Full-Scale Fire Tests on Specific Wall and Ceiling Ma-*

terials of Mobile Home Modules. Washington, D.C.: U.S. Department of Housing and Urban Development.

Technology and Economics (T&E). 1980*a*. *Economic Benefit-Cost and Risk Analysis of Results of Mobile Home Safety Research: Transportation Safety and Durability Analysis.* Washington, D.C.: U.S. Department of Housing and Urban Development.

———. 1980*b*. *Economic Benefit-Cost and Risk Analysis of Results of Mobile Home Safety Research: Wind Safety Analysis.* Washington, D.C.: U.S. Department of Housing and Urban Development.

———. 1980*c*. *Economic Cost-Benefit and Risk Analysis of Results of Mobile Home Safety Research: Fire Safety.* Washington, D.C.: U.S. Department of Housing and Urban Development.

U.S. Fire Administration (USFA). 1980. *Highlights of Fire in the United States.* 2d ed. Washington, D.C. Federal Emergency Management Agency.

Wright, Don. 1981. "Champion Launches Scattered Lot, Subdivision Concepts." *Manufactured Housing DEALER*, January, pp. 42–43.

INDEX

187